Additional Praise for *Success by Ten*

"George Russell uses unforgettable stories to tell the tale of his family's business, and share his principles of success in *Success by Ten*. At a time when there is so much dismay and anger regarding our financial institutions, it's heartening to read the story of a man and a family who did it right—with integrity and a focus on service. George is an outstanding business leader and philanthropist, who makes it clear that a successful business is not about capital formation or strategic planning, but about discipline, hard work, fair play, being creative, taking risks, and above all, how you treat people. If George Russell's principles became best practices for business and beyond, we would have a more prosperous people and a more peaceful world."

— Sam A. Nunn, Co-Chairman and Chief Executive Officer of the Nuclear Threat Initiative, U.S. Senator from Georgia, 1972–1996

"George has lived an incredible life, and his success is a tribute to the virtues he promotes: hard work, determination, and integrity. This book tells the story of how George has used these fundamentals to reach the top—a worthwhile read for anyone curious about what it takes to do things on a big scale."

— William H. Gates, Sr., attorney, philanthropist, and author of *Showing Up for Life: Thoughts on the Gifts of a Lifetime*

"Reading this book reminded me of what I have learned from George Russell, Jr., over the years when we worked as co-chairs of EastWest Institute. The principles that George followed in building a billion-dollar business are equally important in my work as a peace mediator. Nonnegotiable integrity, persistence, patience, hiring smarter people than you, being creative, working hard, sharing credit, recognizing luck, planning transitions, taking risks, and having fun were essential for my success. If these principles would have been followed we would have avoided the present financial crises. I, therefore, warmly recommend this book to everybody."

— President Martti Ahtisaari, Chairman, Crisis Management Initiative, President of Finland 1994–2000, Nobel Peace Prize Laureate 2008

"George Russell's *Success by Ten* is a must read. It's filled with wisdom. His life is a great story, and here he tells you how he did it."
—John C. Whitehead, former Deputy Secretary of State, and recipient of the Presidential Citizens Medal

"In *Success by Ten*, George Russell provides an inspiring account of how one man carefully built one of the world's great financial institutions. His story serves as a welcome antidote to the financial chaos created by too many other financial institutions."
—Carla A. Hills, Chair and CEO of Hills & Company, International Consultants, former Secretary of Housing and Urban Development, and former U.S. Trade Representative

"George Russell teaches the vital principles to success. Russell's relationship-based lessons encourage common sense and integrity in the workplace. This book inspires and instills the wisdom necessary to excel in this global economy."
—David Boren, President, the University of Oklahoma, Governor, Oklahoma, 1975–1979, and U.S. Senator, 1979–1994

"George Russell is a change agent. He revolutionized the pension industry. Early on he mobilized money managers and pension fund managers to discover and invest in emerging markets. He helped key NGOs like the EastWest Institute and the National Bureau of Asian Research achieve new levels of impact and recognition. His approaches are simple, but profound. One needs to throw out a lot of those old management books. *Success by Ten* does for management what Russell has already done in so many other fields. This is an inspiring, profound, and easy read for existing and aspiring leaders alike."
—John Edwin Mroz, President, EastWest Institute

"Every business leader and every political leader in America should read this book. Both business and government should be run by George Russell's *Success by Ten*. This is a marvelously readable book with an incredibly vital message."
—Daniel J. Evans, Governor, Washington State, 1965–1977, U.S. Senator, Washington State, 1983–1989

"George Russell is one of the rare figures of the American investment world—a down-to-earth, scrupulously honest, and humane figure, who ordinary people can understand and trust, and who has, incidentally, been successful because of these qualities. He has captured extremely well in this book his philosophy, his view of people, events and history, and his approach to the world. It is a book that must be read, both as an antidote to all that is rotten in the investment world, and, more importantly, as a series of invaluable lessons in life itself, which one might receive from a father, an uncle, or an elder brother."

—John J. Maresca, Rector, University for Peace, and former U.S. Representative to the Organization for Security and Cooperation in Europe

"Success by Ten is a significant, business-building primer. Every entrepreneur and business leader searching for growth wisdom will find helpful practice examples, good stories, and straight-ahead advice. In addition, George Russell provides insights that go well beyond the arts of strategic risk taking, customer service, and product development—all vital aspects in building a billion dollar global business. George shows us the personal leadership attributes that are required: hard work, integrity, guts, refined intuition, and learned optimism. As a result, readers of this book will enjoy a triple treat: an excellent business growth guide, a lively personal story of the challenges and excitement of the entrepreneurial life, and a clear and potent reminder of why living your good values really matters. Enjoy."

—John O'Neal, author of *The Paradox of Success*

"George Russell is an institution builder who pursues visionary goals: investing enormous pension funds to enhance financial security; spurring economic growth in emerging markets; advising to 'reduce the gap between the haves and the have-nots'; integrating China and Russia into the international economy; enhancing understanding of Islam; and focusing health care on prevention and early detection. In all of these undertakings George has been at once strategic and a nut for the details, generous and loyal, and filled with integrity. What an extraordinary legacy."

—Richard J. Ellings, Co-founder and President, National Bureau of Asian Research

"As we sort through the wreckage of our current economy, we often blame the creative business models and esoteric financial vehicles that were all the rage before the bubble burst. What a great antidote to read George Russell's straightforward tale of success and the lessons he learned along the way. He gives his readers powerful reminders about the core values of business and of life, and why they are still as important as ever."

—Mark A. Emmert, President, University of Washington

"George Russell, seeking to grow the company started by his grandfather, along the way invented a profession—investment management consulting—and created a highly respected major investment management organization. This book tells the story of his creative journey, and spells out the lessons he learned, lessons invaluable to all business people, especially entrepreneurs or those seeking to grow small companies."

—Michael J. Clowes, Editor at Large, *Pensions & Investments* and *InvestmentNews*

"George Russell is a man of many talents, including the capacity to see possibility, the courage to pursuit it, the determination to achieve, and the heart to hold it in perspective. He is gifted with a razor sharp intelligence that 'cuts to the chase,' and translates complexity into principles and ideas that are suddenly crystal clear and easy to understand, yet powerful and important. All of these qualities are evident as one reads, *Success by Ten: George Russell's Top Ten Elements to Building a Billion Dollar Business.* The book is at once a warm, personal memoir, and a valuable, professional handbook because George Russell always has, and always will, lead from the heart; authenticity and integrity are his platform."

—Loren Anderson, President, Pacific Lutheran University

Success by Ten

Success by Ten

GEORGE RUSSELL'S TOP TEN ESSENTIALS TO BUILDING A BILLION DOLLAR BUSINESS

George F. Russell, Jr.

with

Michael Sheldon

WILEY

John Wiley & Sons, Inc.

Published by John Wiley & Sons, Inc., Hoboken, New Jersey.
Published simultaneously in Canada.

For general information on our other products and services or for technical support, please contact our Customer Care Department within the United States at (800) 762–2974, outside the United States at (317) 572–3993 or fax (317) 572–4002.

Wiley also publishes its books in a variety of electronic formats. Some content that appears in print may not be available in electronic books. For more information about Wiley products, visit our web site at www.wiley.com.

Library of Congress Cataloging-in-Publication Data:
Russell, George F., 1932-
   Success by ten : George Russell's top ten essentials to building a billion dollar business/George F. Russell, Jr. with Michael Sheldon.
       p. cm.
   Includes index.
ISBN 978-0-470-53727-5
   1. Pension trusts.   2. Business consultants.   3. Success in
business.   I. Sheldon, Michael, 1952-   II. Title.
      HD7091.R89 2010
      331.25'240684–dc22
                                                          2009025210

Printed in the United States of America
10   9   8   7   6   5   4   3   2   1

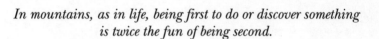

*In mountains, as in life, being first to do or discover something
is twice the fun of being second.*

Robert H. Bates
The Love of Mountains Is Best

Contents

Contents

Contents

Acknowledgment

This book would not have been possible without the sustained efforts of Brian Barker. Brian was Frank Russell Company's first historian. When he joined us in 1980, Brian's first project was to interview people at all levels of the company and create a narrative of the Russell organization. He later moved into sales, where he helped build the clientele, first, for our institutional funds and, later, for our new ventures in private equity. After I retired from Frank Russell Company, Brian helped us build the sales and marketing capabilities at Threshold Group. In 2003, our working relationship came full circle, when I suggested that we build an archive of interviews with key people who shaped the fortunes of Frank Russell Company. Over the next few years, Brian contacted and interviewed more than 80 individuals—most of them Russell associates, but also clients, partners, and even a few competitors. Those conversations are the foundation on which *Success by Ten* is built.

INTRODUCTION

My path to success began with a cold call. That may seem like a startling confession, since many people think of entrepreneurs as having a direct line to venture capitalists. Perhaps it was because, in those early years, I didn't even know what an entrepreneur was! I was looking for clients, not funding, and I made cold calls at the outset because there was no other alternative available.

Throughout my career, I've had my own way of going about things. In 1958, I graduated from Harvard Business School. I never seriously considered staying on the East Coast or seeking a position with an established company. My family was in Tacoma, Washington, and I returned there to work for my grandfather's small mutual fund company, even though the profits were negligible and the number of employees totaled two. My grandfather passed away 90 days after I started, leaving the company to my father. Ten years later, in 1969, I bought Frank Russell Company from my father for $250,000. Over the next 30 years it grew into a global enterprise worth more than $1 billion when sold in 1999.

In retrospect, it looks like I knew what I was doing. In fact, I followed my instincts and learned by trial and error. My way is not textbook; I didn't learn it from the Harvard MBA program, where we worked through case studies about capital formation, strategic planning, and scientific approaches to management.

As you will see, my business success factors don't require a spreadsheet. They are people-focused and motivational. I have no doubt that some people will define them as common sense. All I can say is, if that's true, why doesn't everybody use them?

My way isn't glamorous. It's slow. In fact, it moves at a glacial or evolutionary pace. That said, I believe the principles I developed in creating and growing Frank Russell Company are broadly accessible and can be applied in organizations of any type or size.

These are the lessons I wish I'd been taught in business school. It would have saved me a lot of time and trouble. I hope that these essays on success will help you, the future generations of business leaders, find the right path more quickly and easily than I did.

GEORGE F. RUSSELL, JR.
September 2009

CHAPTER

1

Non-Negotiable Integrity

"DO THE RIGHT THING."

Before you are a successful businessperson, you need to be a person. By that I mean a certain kind of person—a person with strong core values and, most importantly, integrity.

It was my grandfather, Frank Russell, who was my first model of integrity, and that's where my personal story begins.

Frank had worked on Wall Street, but decided to retire after the Crash. He came home to Tacoma in 1936 at the age of 58. My grandmother was sickly, so she and my grandfather, Frank, lived with us at times, or else in a nice house just down the block. Frank founded a mutual fund company called Bondstock, which you'll hear about in Chapter 2.

Right now, I want to focus on the fact that Frank was present for me, throughout my childhood, on a daily basis. My father, George, on the other hand, was a workaholic. He ran several businesses, and puttered in the basement in his "spare" time. In fact, he was an inventor who accumulated more than 100 patents. The by-product of his work was that I ended up having Frank as my closest family influence.

And Frank was a man of integrity. I don't mean that he preached it. He never lectured or indulged in parables or abstractions. We simply spent a lot of time together; all of it was what's now called "quality time"; and I came out of the family home with the experience of knowing an upright man whom I loved and respected.

Frank was also highly respected in the community for the way he conducted his business. After he died, I took over his business and his clientele. A lot of the investors in Bondstock were local people and one of them was a rough-looking, gruff-talking commercial fisherman, who wandered into the office one morning. Our receptionist found him so intimidating that she called in John James, a promising young executive I had recently managed to lure away from Bank of New York. John retired just a few years ago after more than 35 years with the company; as he tells it:

> I came out and introduced myself. Without saying anything, this man reaches into his pocket, whips out $15,000 in cash and throws it on the desk. He had just come back from fishing in Alaska. He said, "Invest it for me."
>
> I said, "Where would you like to invest it?"
>
> "Go ask George Junior," he said. "He'll know where I want my money." And he started for the door.
>
> I called out after him, "Can we give you a receipt...?"
>
> "If I need a receipt," he said, "this company's changed and I want my money back."

You can see why my grandfather became my first role model. He founded his business on trust and integrity, and I simply did my best to copy him.

Building Character

I met my second role model in high school. My parents sent me back east in 1946 to attend Philips Exeter. Prior to leaving, I'd been diagnosed with a heart murmur and counseled never to do anything that would get my heart rate up. That's a pretty stiff sentence for a 14-year-old.

Fortunately, when I got to Exeter, I landed in a dorm supervised by Robert H. Bates. Even back then, at the age of 35, Bob was a world-class mountaineer. He had helped to map the Canadian Yukon for the National Geographic Society and was the first to climb 17,147-foot Mount Lucania, which had been the highest unscaled peak in North America.

In 1938, Bob and his friend, Charlie Houston, put together an expedition to climb K2. That's the secondhighest mountain in the world and a more difficult technical challenge than Mt. Everest. Nobody managed to conquer K2 until 1954—a year later than Everest—and only 280 people have ever summited K2, compared to 10 times that many for Everest. Obviously, Bob and Charlie didn't succeed in 1938. But they got to within 1,000 feet of the summit before turning back for lack of adequate supplies of food and matches to melt drinking water.

Now, imagine what Bob must have thought when he first caught sight of me, a homesick 14-year-old who'd been told never to exert himself or get too excited. I was about to say "Bob took me under his wing," but it'd be the wrong metaphor. In fact, he pushed me out of the nest. He told me to go see Charlie Houston, who at that time happened to have a medical practice right there in Exeter. Charlie listened to my heart for about five minutes. Then he said, "Forget it. Go to work. Get busy. Do things."

That's exactly what I did. I joined the wrestling team—a sport I pursued with some success throughout high school and college. (My wrestling weight was 137 pounds.)

And, now that I had my "Get Out of Jail Free Card," Bob didn't waste any time getting me involved in mountaineering. Together we set up the Exeter Mountaineering Club. I was its President for four years, and what a terrific experience that was! Bob took us up to the White Mountains in New Hampshire and to the cliffs by the ocean. We learned all of the fundamental mountaineering skills, such as how to rappel and how to save a climbing partner if he happened to slip.

Looking back over the years, I consider my time with Bob as the cornerstone of my education. He pushed me out into the world with all its risks and challenges and, in doing so, introduced me to the rewards of proving yourself in the natural world and in competition with other people.

When you think about it, both mountaineering and wrestling test your integrity in unique ways. To climb a mountain, you either have it or you don't. Physically, mentally, you'll know whether you have the strength to take another step forward, or that it's time to turn around and head home. There's no possibility of cheating. When you succeed, your spirit soars and you gain confidence. When you fail, it's disappointing, but you gain experience. You establish a personal benchmark that you can try to exceed the next time. You understand that failure is not the end; it's the beginning of a new opportunity. As Bob and Charlie put it in *Five Miles High*:

> Men who climb mountains go in humility to try their skill and knowledge against wind and cold, great heights and far distances. They know that the contest purges them of artificialities, returning them to their homes refreshed. Having faced life stripped to essentials, they can better appreciate and properly evaluate the luxuries of civilization.

Wrestling presents a different challenge. You pit your strength and stamina and wiles against someone who is as much like you as possible. The weight differentials in wrestling are usually only a pound or so at the most. There can be no excuses on account of your competitors' inherent physical advantages. There's no equipment involved and no teammates to pick up the slack or let you down. It's just you and the other guy. The umpire is right on top of every move, so it's virtually impossible to cheat. Does wrestling teach non-negotiable integrity? You'd better believe it.

Reach for the Summit

Mountains, and mountain climbing, have long symbolized challenges—such as spiritual quests and the attainment of excellence. Frank Russell Company is situated in the shadow of Mount

Rainier, so "the mountain" as we call it was the logical symbol for our logo, as well as our advertising when we finally got around to it.

For anyone in the investment management business, the summit is a nice metaphor for the goal of long-term investing. Individuals want to be able to maintain their standard of living in retirement, or whatever else they aspire to. For pension funds, it's the ability to pay for employee benefits—to keep up their end of the pension promise. Foundations spread the benefits of health, wealth, culture, and so forth. And some university endowments have been so successful in their investment programs that they are, just now, acting on their ability to significantly lower, if not eliminate, tuition for many of their students. Wrap all of these types of clients into one package and you have the Frank Russell Company mission: *Improving financial security for people.* That's the mountain we try to climb every day.

Surprisingly, wrestling also has an interesting analog in the investment business. As a consultant, our first assignment was to identify and select investment managers for pension funds. Back in 1969, when we started, it was typical for a corporate treasurer or CFO to simply call in whichever bank the company happened to be borrowing from and give them the complete mandate for investing the pension fund assets. In those days, it was a relationship-based system.

Our value proposition was that clients would benefit by moving to an objective, measurement-based system of choosing managers for their pension funds. To deliver on our promise, however, we had to invent tools that would allow us to accurately compare managers. It all seems obvious in hindsight, but we needed better benchmarks, style analysis, and performance universes.

Otherwise, it would be like asking a 137-pound wrestler to go up against someone in the 160-pound weight class. In other words, a large part of our contribution to the industry was helping to figure out the right "weight classifications" for managers: That was the only way we could decide who was really doing a better job.

In this respect, you could say that integrity wasn't just a standard of behavior for employees—or "associates" as we always called them—but really the philosophical core of our business. Let me give you a couple of examples of how non-negotiable integrity was vital to the success of our business.

Our Business is Based on Trust

First I'll describe what it was like researching institutional money managers back in 1969. In those days, pension assets were concentrated in relatively few trust banks and insurance company fixed-income products. These were grand old institutions, where the bankers sometimes acted as though they were doing their clients a favor by accepting their money. Even a corporate treasurer at a blue-chip corporation, in charge of a multimillion-dollar pension, might have felt uncomfortable asking too many questions about process or performance.

Madelyn Smith, who was our first director of equity research, describes the scene when she began researching managers in London, where traditions were even more relationship-based than in New York, if possible. Madelyn recalls,

> We would visit the Merchant Banks and they all had ornate dining rooms and their own chefs. They would serve a three-course lunch with wine and tell you that they had been in business for 200 years; that they had all these assets under management; that they were from very solid educational backgrounds. And they seemed to assume that we would, of course, recommend them to our clients.
>
> After lunch we would try to carry on a more direct conversation. We asked questions that people of good breeding would never ask. We'd grill them about their investment process, and they agonized over giving us performance data. No doubt these Merchant Bankers thought we were brash Americans.

In fairness to the money managers, we were subjecting them to something they had never experienced before. Over time, many grew to appreciate the process and we'd start to hear comments like, "You understand us better than we understand ourselves."

But in the early days, it's easy to see why some firms might have been uncomfortable opening their doors to a virtually unknown firm that was requiring that they explain their trade secrets. That took a lot of trust on their part, as they knew we would also be talking to their competitors. Of course, the assets that our clients commanded were a significant enticement. But without integrity our business simply would not have worked. The managers had to believe that they would be treated fairly; that they would be analyzed on objective criteria; and, most importantly, that their confidential information would be scrupulously guarded.

Integrity also played a central role when we launched our investment management business. We understood that our core consulting clients might have concerns about our introducing a new area of focus, so I traveled and talked to each client, face to face. It took me three weeks to do that. I asked them what they thought. Most said that our knowledge of managers was our core bread-and-butter business and they understood why we would want to leverage that. Only three out of 40 said they were worried: "You will make more money in the funds business than you do in the consulting business and you will dilute your attention to us."

I gave them my word of honor that we would not do that. I promised, "I will come back five years from now and I will prove it to you." Of course, I went back more frequently than that. But five years later they were still clients and continued to be happy with the relationship.

In fact, our consulting business continued to develop over time. We expanded our roster *slightly*, to 45 major corporations, whose assets grew *phenomenally*—representing more than $1 trillion in assets as of 2008. As the assets grew, so did the awareness within these organizations that professionals were needed on staff to fulfill their fiduciary responsibility. In 1969, only the treasurer was paying attention to the pension plan. Now these corporations all have major teams of highly sophisticated investment professionals.

Our clients' increasing ability to perform more of the work themselves changed the dynamic of our relationship. We knew

Russell had to develop new capabilities that were of value for them or we'd never have a job. They would fire us. The Russell organization remained highly motivated to serve its consulting clients. Over time, we developed more sophisticated, better ways of selecting managers. We pioneered new asset classes, including international and real estate in the 1970s and private equity and alternative strategies in the 1990s. And we built a next-generation asset liability modeling system, capable of handling multiple time periods and different definitions of risk. Most of these innovations eventually worked their way into the funds, but the necessity of keeping ahead of the curve with our consulting clients was always the spark.

Now we can look back and take satisfaction in the fact that we've had 30-year anniversary celebrations with many of our original clients. But in 1980, the outcome was in doubt, and we really needed the support we received from our consulting clients, particularly when it came to dealing with the press. Some money managers whom we were researching for our consulting clients stated strong concerns that we would be competing with them in our fund business. Other observers felt it would be a conflict of interest for us to recommend managers to consulting clients and also hire the same or different managers as sub-advisors to our funds.

I explained to the press that, first, we did not recommend our own funds to the consulting clients, so that wasn't a conflict, and second, the managers in the funds were not paying us to get the assets—*we* were paying *them*. Also there was a significant difference based on the size of the pension fund: We made customized recommendations for the large plans that could meet the managers' minimums. The only way the smaller plans could access many of these managers was through our commingled funds.

Criticisms were floating around for about 18 months. But the fact that we had the support of the consulting clients enabled us to keep our heads up. I kept restating that there was no conflict and eventually people began to accept that. Again it boils down to integrity. We could never have moved into the asset management side of our business without the trust of our original clients.

Integrity is More Important than the Bottom Line

It's not enough to have integrity *most* of the time, because even a single exception can kill you. That's why I always talk about *non-negotiable integrity*. Strictly speaking, it's probably redundant. But in our world where everything, including values, is viewed in relative terms, I feel it's necessary to make it clear that integrity is *absolute*. It's either 100 percent or it's not integrity.

A panel I attended at the Economic Forum in Davos reinforced this point for me. One area of focus at Davos was Global Competitiveness. A panel of CEOs explored the topic: What are the characteristics that allow an organization to last—not just for decades—but centuries? Two of the companies represented were British Petroleum and Westinghouse—no strangers to controversy. I was fascinated to see the conclusion. The panel agreed that companies that paid most of their attention to the bottom line would fail. The companies that have the best chance of long-term success are the ones that are honest and accept a set of core values.

It's not hard to see why. The downfall of Barings Bank in 1995 was brought on by the illicit trading activities of a single employee. Over decades, Barings' executives had made thousands of business decisions and taken countless risks. As Great Britain's oldest merchant bank, they had financed the Napoleonic Wars and the Louisiana Purchase. But they couldn't survive dishonesty within.

Today, the press amplifies the consequences of any misstep or perceived impropriety. Bad news gets front-page treatment. The correction goes on page 14, below the fold. Former Labor Secretary Ray Donovan's rueful comment, "Which office do I go to to get my reputation back?" is simply a fact of life for anyone whose work is subject to public scrutiny.

Do the Right Thing

At Frank Russell Company, we felt that simply obeying the law wasn't enough and that industry ethics simply enshrines a herd mentality. We wanted to set the bar a bit higher, so, as part of our culture, we talked about "doing the right thing." It's closely related to non-negotiable integrity; you might say it's the proactive version.

In the mid-1990s, Lynn Anderson was president and CEO of our investment management business. Lynn is a smart and talented executive, with a sense of humor as dry as the plains of Kansas where he hails from. We initially brought him in because of his tremendous leadership and fund operations expertise. Now he was in my office with a couple of members of his team, trying to sort out a difficult problem.

We had launched a real estate equity fund that was experiencing temporary liquidity problems tied to the market slump in the early 1990s. This was a unique vehicle at the time, providing direct ownership of commercial property in a commingled fund. Possibly some of the clients weren't used to the format. In any case, the fund had a queue for redemptions, which we paid out whenever properties were sold. Some clients complained about their position in the queue; they wanted cash right away.

It took Lynn and his associates quite a while, a half hour or more, to explain the situation and the different options for dealing with it. Frankly, I barely listened to a word they were saying. I was thinking about Russia at the time—specifically, how would they handle the transition to a market economy?

When Lynn finished, I said, "Thanks for telling me that. Incidentally, if a reporter got wind of this, what would you want to see on the front page of the *Wall Street Journal* tomorrow?"

There was dead silence. They just got up and left.

Later, Lynn told me he got on a plane with a couple of checks, paid directly from our company account, that he hand-delivered to the clients. He said the amount of money wasn't that significant, but it seemed to make a big difference to the clients. Lynn did the right thing.

As a side note, I'm not sure the clients in the queue did the right thing. When the real estate market turned around, as it inevitably would several years later, that fund performed like gangbusters.

Integrity Cannot Be Negotiable

We didn't have too many integrity issues during my time at Russell. As I said, we made it clear that integrity was non-negotiable. It wasn't three strikes and you're out. Our policy on integrity issues, things that could potentially affect the entire enterprise, was that you'd have one strike and that was it. It happened only once. One fellow had been with us for 15 years prior to his misbehavior, which wasn't something that a typical corporation would see as cause for terminating the person. But we did.

There was no argument from him; he knew it was non-negotiable. And we didn't make an announcement or publish it.

But word gets around pretty fast. And so you begin to build the expectation of a behavior pattern that includes a high level of ethics, honesty, and keeping things in plain sight—nothing's under the table.

This may sound punitive, but really our culture was very people-friendly in almost every way. As I said, we didn't have many integrity issues over the years. A large part of that had to do with the way we hired people. To succeed at Frank Russell Company requires a special kind of person. In the first place, our location in Tacoma is not for everyone. If you like the outdoors, particularly a bit of mountaineering or sailing, then you're in paradise. But if you're addicted to the bustle of Manhattan, you're probably not going to find a suitable place in the Pacific Northwest. So we always first brought people out here, so they could get a good feel for the place.

On our end, we also wanted people to get a strong exposure to the culture. So we'd arrange a series of interviews—as many as a dozen. We figured if you ran the gauntlet of that many people, you'd get a pretty good flavor of how we operate. At that point, you'd be either very excited about joining us, or wanting to get away—as far and as fast as you could.

So, a rigorous vetting process was the first step in indoctrinating associates into the Russell culture. But you can't just put it out there once and forget about it. We also knew it was important to make certain that the basic culture of the company was talked about on a regular basis by as many people as possible. We used to keep saying it in the hallways; we used to keep talking about it. Because unless you do that it will eventually fade away.

I no longer have any official role at Russell Investments, as the company is now known, but of course they're just down the street. Occasionally, someone in senior management will ask if I have any thoughts about how to run the company. When that comes up, I always advise them to make sure that the basic culture is talked about and believed by everybody. That's number one. And it's probably all they need to hear from me. The reason is that subscribing to core values is the best way to ensure the longevity of the organization.

Of course, there are short-term benefits as well. When you're part of an organization whose number-one rule is non-negotiable integrity, you're not worried about your colleagues—they're all honest people.

In fact, that might make a good academic project for you: See whether you can quantify the productivity advantage resulting from non-negotiable integrity.

Key Points from Chapter 1

1. Core values will sustain a company over time; focusing on the bottom line will not.
2. Integrity, the core value at Frank Russell Company, was central to our core competency of objectively measuring managers. We could not have built our business without it.
3. Integrity must be non-negotiable. One slip can ruin the entire enterprise.
4. It's not enough to simply obey the law. *Doing the right thing* cements relationships and is the best PR strategy.
5. Take the time to carefully vet new employees and make sure everyone supports your core values.

CHAPTER

2

Persistence, Patience, and Cold Calls

"IT TOOK 11 YEARS TO FIND THE RESTROOM."

I am a peddler and, as I mentioned at the outset, everything we achieved at Frank Russell Company began with a cold call. However, I had to work for 11 years—from 1958, when I graduated from Harvard Business School, until 1969—before I was ready and able to make that call. That's why, when I say, "It took me 11 years to find the restroom," Frank Russell Company associates understand that I'm talking about the early days of the company, after my grandfather died, when my business was selling the Bondstock mutual fund to individual investors in the Pacific Northwest.

Finding the restroom, of course, marked the beginning of the pension fund consulting business, and I suppose you have to think like a peddler to appreciate the metaphor. It only requires a bit of imagination: Just consider how you'd feel after spending days in airports, visiting strange cities—particularly the canyons of lower Manhattan, where there's a Sabrett's hot dog cart on every corner, but an accessible restroom is a scarce commodity.

A peddler's path to entrepreneurial success may not be the quickest way to get there. I don't consider myself a *visionary*, but rather someone who had an *evolutionary* approach to building a business. The difference is pretty clear-cut: I don't think you can turn yourself into a visionary; at least it's not something I can teach you. But I can show you how to become an evolutionary entrepreneur. It takes persistence and patience. And it helps if you're willing to make cold calls.

The perfect example of a visionary entrepreneur is Jeff Bezos, founder of Amazon.com. In the early 1990s, Jeff was working in New York, creating software for a hedge fund. The Internet was taking off and Jeff recognized an opportunity. He asked himself, "What can I sell online?" and, after considering all the options, settled on books. Then he asked, "Where should I locate this business?" He chose Seattle, based on the availability of software engineers and proximity to a book-distribution center in Oregon.

Of course, the visionary still has plenty of work to do. Implementation is never trivial. But the initial idea for the business comes quickly, and the visionary is able to start executing right away. It's top-down thinking followed by giant steps toward a clearly defined goal.

The evolutionary model is just the reverse: Thinking is bottom up. As a salesman, I was learning about the market—one cold call, one meeting, one piece of data at a time. Every step was a baby step. It was trial and error for years and, when the goal finally appeared, it was still at a great distance and shrouded in mist.

Early Days at Frank Russell Company

My father George was much more successful at business than my grandfather Frank. He worked as the business manager for the Tacoma daily newspaper, which was owned by his father-in-law, Frank Baker, and is now known as the *Tacoma News Tribune*. He had a second venture that was an outlet for his inventiveness, Mann-Russell Electronics. He also started the West Tacoma

Newsprint Company, which became a great success after World War II ended.

When I returned to Tacoma in 1958, my father wanted me to go to work either for the *Tribune* or Mann-Russell Electronics, but I wanted to work for my grandfather at Frank Russell Company. You have to understand that there wasn't much there. In 1958, there were 36 stockholders who had a combined $300,000 in assets. That works out to about $8,600 per investor, which was very small even in those days. I'm sure my dad looked at his dad's operation as virtually nothing and therefore reasoned, *What's the future there?*

But I felt that special bond with my grandfather, so I went to work at Frank Russell Company in July 1958. I was the third employee, after Frank and his part-time secretary, Rachel Hagmann. He'd been in the same office since 1936. It was about 15 feet across and 20 feet long, and there wasn't even enough room for a third desk.

I went out and knocked on doors, trying to sell shares in Bondstock. That's how I started. Then in October my grandfather passed away. He was 80 years old. I persuaded Rachel to come to work full time, so I could keep the headcount up to two.

I took over Frank's desk. I remember vividly how Rachel pointed out that the desk was too high for me, and she suggested that we buy a new chair that could adjust its height. I told her I was sorry we couldn't do that, because we couldn't afford it. I said, "Go get a saw," and I cut off about three inches from each of the desk's wooden legs, and it worked just fine.

Building a Retail Sales Operation

Through persistence, patience and, yes, quite a few cold calls, I eventually built a retail sales force of about 350 people. Approximately 80 percent of them were part time. We were copying what a lot of other organizations were doing in those days, which was selling term insurance and investing the difference in mutual funds. Term insurance was a new product that was gradually becoming popular. The premiums for term insurance are a lot less than for whole life. And people were beginning to hear about mutual funds and starting to think that maybe they should invest. Our pitch was that people would not be paying more out of pocket; all they were doing was changing from a high-cost premium to a low-cost premium, and investing the difference in a mutual fund.

We did business in Washington, Oregon, Idaho, and Alaska— an enormous territory geographically. Fortunately, I'd had a lot of extra time in the military, so I'd taken flying lessons and earned my pilot's license. That came in handy with one of our salesmen, who lived outside of Wenatchee, in Eastern Washington. I used to drive to Ellensburg and then across the mountains up north to meet him. That was a pain in the neck; it took too much time. So I decided to fly instead.

I'd drive to the airfield in Ellensburg and pick up a very light single-engine airplane. That was all I could afford. It didn't have the power to fly directly over the mountains: I had to circle about 20 times to get high enough to slip across the top of those mountains, then come in circles down. I'd fly around this man's farmhouse as a signal that he should meet me at the Wenatchee airport. Then I would land the plane and we'd have our sales meeting. We'd talk about whose doors he'd been knocking on and techniques to increase his production.

In due course, I obviously needed a sales manager. I asked around and kept hearing about a fellow by the name of Dick Lothrop, who lived in Bellevue, Washington, and was working for one of the big mutual fund companies.

I heard that he had worked for three different firms and in each case he'd become the organization's best salesman. I called and made an appointment to meet him at his house in Bellevue. Then it occurred to me that I was about to meet someone who was the big producer for a national organization. In those days, I was driving an elderly Chevy coupe, which wouldn't look too good coming up in front of his house.

So, I called my friend Paul Titus, who ran the Ford dealership in Tacoma, and I borrowed a brand-new Thunderbird; it was copper-colored, with a vinyl top. Later on, Dick's wife, Shirley, told me that when she saw the Thunderbird drive up, she said to Dick, "Well, at least he's coming in a fancy car. . . ."

Dick and I talked nonstop for about five hours. We spoke by phone the next day, and Dick said, "Have you made your decision?" I said, "You're hired," and he said, "Okay, let's go to work."

It happened that fast. Dick was always a good negotiator and part of the deal was that he'd get a Thunderbird just like mine. I didn't want to admit at the outset about borrowing the Thunderbird, so I had to go back to Paul Titus and buy *two* Thunderbirds—one for myself and one for Dick. It was probably a year later when I told him what actually had happened. But that was a big expense for me. Especially when you consider that I was only paying myself about $300 per month.

Those two T-Birds may have been a big expense, but they were also one of the best investments I ever made. Dick Lothrop brought to the table a set of skills in marketing, direct selling, and cold calling that I knew nothing about. Those skills proved to be essential a few years later when I eventually found the restroom. I can state categorically that without that sales education from Dick, I could not have succeeded during the period from 1969 to 1974, when I was establishing my consulting clientele. I was making 25 sales calls in five days, in five cities, every other week, for about four years. Without the knowledge Dick provided—to me in particular but also to the entire organization—we probably never would have succeeded the way we did in getting major corporations to sign up for a brand-new idea.

Harvard to the Rescue

Dick Lothrop definitely energized the sales force. But he couldn't change the fact that there wasn't significant upside to our business model of selling term insurance and investing the difference in mutual funds. Lots of other organizations were doing it, and we weren't constructing an organization that had any future in terms of building its impact or increasing its profits.

Basically, I was getting bored. Then Harvard came to the rescue. It was in June 1969, when Harvard Business School staged an all-day retreat in Seattle. It was the first time they'd ever done that—and it was at the Seattle Center, the site of the Space Needle and the 1962 World's Fair. The retreat was scheduled on a Saturday, and I thought I had better stay home with my wife, Jane, and the kids. But Jane insisted that I attend.

Looking back, that was a critically important position for her to take, because it was the first step on the path toward pension fund consulting.

There were about 2,000 people at the retreat and I don't remember what the morning discussion topics were. We broke for lunch in a big hall. I headed toward the back and happened to sit next to a man who had an ID tag on his lapel that said, "Assistant to the Chairman at LTV." LTV stood for Ling-Temco-Vought, which, at the time, was in the top 20 of the Fortune 500. Its chairman, Jim Ling, had assembled an innovative conglomerate that included one of the nation's biggest steel manufacturers, an airline, a meat processor, and so on. Jim Ling was definitely high profile, making regular appearances on the covers of *BusinessWeek* and *Time*. When I read the agenda, I learned that he was going to be the guest speaker at lunch.

And so, by absolute coincidence, I had happened to sit next to the personal assistant of Mr. Ling, one of the biggest names in business. We introduced ourselves, and I let him know—discreetly, politely, but without beating around the bush—that I was in the investment business. He mentioned the fact that LTV had just lost the person that ran their $150 million pension fund and he asked if I might be in a position to help them find his replacement.

It was as if destiny was handing me Opportunity—with a capital *O*—on a silver platter. But I was still a mutual fund peddler, and $150 million was several decimal places bigger than anything I had ever sold before. So, naturally, I replied, "You should buy some mutual funds instead." He looked at me kind of funny and I knew I had only a couple of minutes before they served lunch.

I used that opportunity—with a small *o*—to give him a short pitch on why he should use mutual funds. Finally, he said, "That's interesting; why don't you come down and tell that to Jim Ling?"

We made an appointment for me to meet Jim Ling at LTV's headquarters in Dallas in about a week. I remember that I went down there on a Sunday. I had worn tennis shoes on the plane and forgot to put business shoes in my suitcase, and my meeting was at 8:30 the next morning.

So, there I was, walking the streets of downtown Dallas early on a Monday morning, dressed in a business suit and tennis shoes, frantically searching for a shoe store. Fortunately, the city still had a lot of stores downtown; they hadn't all gone out to the malls yet. Around eight o'clock, I saw a light in the back of a shoe store, and the proprietor responded when he heard me banging on the door. Properly shod, I was able to make it to my meeting on time.

Still, it was a bit intimidating. At the time, the LTV building was the tallest building in Dallas, which reflected Jim Ling's—and the company's—status in the business community.

I was 37 years old, and that was still considered young in those days. I confess I was a bit scared going in to see this very important businessman. I had a vision of an office that was 100 yards long and 50 yards wide, with a desk that was six feet tall. That was all fantasy, of course. They also told me that I had six minutes with him—max.

I gave him my pitch on mutual funds and then I slammed my hand down on his desk and said, "What do you think? Was it a strikeout, foul out, or a home run?" He just looked at me and said, "Tell it to the board next month."

I thanked him and left. Later, his assistant told me that nobody had ever slammed their hand on his desk. I'm not sure where that came from. Maybe I'd learned it from Dick Lothrop— I really don't remember. In any case, I had a month to prepare my pitch for the board.

Up until that time, the record for the highest annual sales for mutual funds belonged to a woman in Houston, Texas, who had sold $5 million worth of mutual funds each year for several years running. My meeting with LTV's board went well, as did subsequent meetings with Textron and General Telephone. Together, these three sales established a new record, I believe, of $50 million worth of mutual fund sales in a three-month period.

The Cold Call

Once those three corporations had a significant investment in mutual funds in their pension portfolios, our job was to monitor the results. Obviously, I was having conversations with the people in charge of the pension funds, and these reinforced the idea that came up during that first coincidental chat with Jim Ling's assistant. Big corporations were definitely looking for help in finding the right people to manage their pension assets, but mutual funds weren't really the ideal solution for them. They were looking for something more tailored to their specific needs. After 11 years, the idea had nearly completed its evolution. But there was one big obstacle remaining: how to overcome the deeply ingrained status quo.

I mentioned in the first chapter that in those days pension funds typically gave their assets to the trust department of a large local bank with which they already had a relationship. Mike Clowes, who edited the pension industry's trade publication, *Pensions & Investments*, for 30 years beginning in 1973, nicely illuminates the challenge I faced in his invaluable book, *The Money Flood*.[1] Mike cites the 1971 edition of the *Money Market Directory*, which reported on 2,450 pension funds in existence at that time, with assets totaling $160 billion. That might seem like a large list of prospects until you consider the fact that:

> . . . Most of the largest pension funds still had only bank managers, and many only one bank manager. The 1971 *Money Market Directory* showed that Morgan Guaranty Trust Co. of New York was the single most popular fund management organization; it was employed by 129 companies or public employee plans. Next came Chase Manhattan Bank with

114 clients, and Bankers Trust Co., New York, with 106. Most of the other plans were overseen by local trust banks. In the Pittsburgh area, Mellon Bank was the dominant pension fund manager. In Chicago, Harris Trust and Savings Bank and First National Bank of Chicago dominated. On the West Coast, Bank of America, Wells Fargo Bank and Trust, and Crocker National Bank fought it out. Companies generally employed the banks from which they received their financing.[2]

Those were old, established names. But were they really the best at managing money? And if they were good at managing equities, did it follow that they were equally good at fixed income? Clearly, it would take methodical research to find out.

Because I had just convinced my three new clients to buy mutual funds, it simply wasn't possible to go back to them a few months later telling them to sell their mutual funds and replace them with a manager or two or three. I had to go to somewhere else to try the idea of selecting managers.

One day, I asked Rachel to get me a copy of the JCPenney S&P sheet. The S&P sheet in those days was a single page of data for each publicly traded corporation, with the name and phone number of the chief financial officer (CFO) on the back.

I'll never know why I picked JCPenney. Possibly, I had driven by their store on the way to work that day. I really don't remember. The fact remains that I picked JCPenney out of the blue and dialed the number for the chief financial officer. But he was out of town. That turned out to be a lucky break. I found out later that both the CFO and the CEO had a relationship with one of the big banks that was managing all of their pension assets. If I had tried to talk to the CFO about splitting the responsibility among several managers, he probably would have hung up on me.

Instead, the secretary transferred the call to the corporate treasurer, whose name was Paul Kaltinick. Now, I didn't know Paul Kaltinick from Adam. But he got on the phone and I asked him point blank if he thought a single manager could be the best at all types of investing—equity and fixed income. That started a seven-minute conversation that included the idea that I wanted to do the research and help him select managers for the JCPenney pension fund.

Paul asked me when I would be in New York and I told him, "next week." I put down the phone and explained what had just happened to my assistant. She immediately contacted the travel agent to make reservations for New York. I met Paul in his office the following week; we talked for about 45 minutes and he basically hired me on the spot.

Paul Kaltinick's Perspective

That's my recollection. But the client is always right, so here is Paul's version:

> George came in and we spoke for probably an hour and a half. Penney had started its pension fund in 1967. Prior to that it was just Penney stock—much like Sears Roebuck. I was the treasurer at the time the pension fund was set up and was involved on a committee of three who had selected two banks to manage the fund. At the point in time when George called, it happened that we were about to replace one of the banks, because they were doing a terrible job.
>
> I'd begun collecting names of firms to interview, using the "scientific" approach that all corporate treasurers relied on in those days. They would get on the phone with their fellow corporate treasurers and ask, "Who's managing your fund? Are you happy with them? Do you know any other firms?"
>
> I had compiled a list of 19 names, and I was about to start calling to determine which ones I should visit. I described all this to George and he said, "Why don't you give me the 19 names? I'll visit these firms and then prepare an individual report on each one, with my recommendation as to whether they should be considered or not."

As you can see, we were already thinking along the same lines about the need for selecting managers based on merit.

However, working out our business arrangement was a bit more complicated.

> I said that sounded interesting, but wondered what was in it for Frank Russell Company. George said, "I'm seeking to build up clients and this is a low-cost way for you to start."
>
> I wasn't sure whether he had won our business or not and I told him, "You understand of course, that you can do this work and still not get hired." He said, "Yes, I'm willing to take that chance."
>
> So that was our initial agreement. He said he could get it done in three weeks. We opened our calendars and set a date, and off he went. Subsequently, I met with the pension committee and described what had transpired. We were all pretty interested in how this new service was going to work out.

It was interesting for me as well. I can tell you that was one exciting plane ride back to Tacoma, as I studied Paul's list and began working out my plan of attack for researching managers.

> Three weeks later, George Russell showed up at my door, report in hand. It evaluated the firms, manager by manager—with a few exceptions. Some of the original 19 didn't have a full report because George didn't feel they were worth considering, and he briefly listed the reasons why. From the 19 names, he singled out two or three that deserved close consideration. He also mentioned a number of newer firms that had been formed in the last several years that deserved some consideration, and would I be interested in hearing about those? I said "yes," and so he presented five additional firms for us to consider.

A Unique Selling Proposition

That's the story of my cold call. You can see how, with a result like that, you might come to believe—as I do—that cold calling is a good use of your time.

To me, it's interesting to think that Paul Kaltinick had been given the responsibility for the JCPenney pension fund only six months earlier. They had hired a couple of managers, one of which was underperforming, which led Paul to have the same gut feeling I was having: this fundamental idea that it was wrong to assume that one manager could be the best at a variety of different asset classes. That just seemed like an improbable reach.

I believe that Paul had this notion in his head without fully defining it. And I was less than half a step ahead of him, saying, "Let's find the best manager for U.S. equities. Let's find the best manager for U.S. fixed income. And let's base our decisions on research—purely on merit, as well as we can define it."

Paul connected with that idea and JCPenney became our first client. Of course, when you start out like this you have to offer a service that doesn't cost very much; the initial consulting fee was very low, somewhere in the range of $30,000 a year.

Over the next few months, the value proposition for our manager research service gradually became more distinct. I could see that if a pension fund paid careful attention to picking managers, they should be able to increase the returns on the pension fund. That would cut down the need for cash flow into the pension fund by the corporation. Obviously, if you were a treasurer or CFO, that's something you would want to accomplish as often as possible, as it'd have a measurable positive impact on bottom-line results.

These thoughts were filtering through my head and it started to dawn on me that this consulting business could actually work because it was very, very saleable! From a peddler's point of view, you couldn't find a stronger argument to get the interest of the people running the financial affairs of major corporations.

Evolving the Business Model

But there were still a few details I needed to work out. As I explained above, when we first started working for JCPenney, we completed the first assignment rather quickly. I helped them pick a couple of managers, whom they hired toward the end of that year. Then Paul said, "Well, thanks very much—you're done." And he said goodbye.

Well, he *tried* to say goodbye. The words hit me like a shock, because I thought we had developed an ongoing relationship. I was stuttering as I tried to explain the notion that now we had to keep track of the managers' performance; we had to decide what to do if they performed better than average, what to do if they performed worse than average, and how to go about it if we had to replace one of them.

I said it was important to stay in close contact, so that Penney would be able to make any needed changes in a timely manner, or to add a new manager if the opportunity presented itself. Paul thought it over and agreed to keep us on for another year if we agreed to cut our original fee in half. During the next year we did hire another manager, but at the end of the year he said the same thing again: "Now you're done."

And I argued with him again, and he agreed to keep us on. It was shaky for a while there, until of course it finally evolved into a permanent relationship.

Compensation

Another important part of the business model that arose right at the beginning was the issue of paying for our consulting services by directing trades from JCPenney's portfolio with "soft dollars" from brokerage commissions. Again, I'll let Paul Kaltinick describe it in his own words:

> We were talking about compensation and George said, "The name of my company is Frank Russell, and this is what we call the Capital Placement division. That means we help you place your capital, and what we want is the brokerage from those transactions. So, when you terminate your bank, those securities have to be sold, and we want to be able to sell them for you, and use the brokerage commissions to compensate ourselves for our work."

I took a deep breath and said, "You know, that doesn't sound real kosher to me. I don't think we will be willing to do something like that." We talked about it for a while, and he explained all the reasons why it was logical and ethical. I listened and said, "I understand everything that you've said, except that it still doesn't pass the smell test to me, but if you like I can try it on my committee members, who are much more conservative than I am."

Paul's reservations are interesting historically. As the industry was so new, you couldn't really say this was the "standard practice." However, performance measurement firms such as A. G. Becker and O'Brien Associates were also taking their compensation in the form of directed brokerage. We started out working for JCPenney on a fixed-fee basis, until they became more comfortable in the relationship. Later, as Paul recalls:

We subsequently agreed to a directed commission arrangement, once we were able to satisfy ourselves that it would be appropriate. Initially we only directed commissions for the purchases, instead of both sides of each trade. In today's environment, with Frank Russell Securities, that would be a very smart deal. But in those days, we didn't have the same commission structure.

This was ironic because, not long after JCPenney's pension committee decided it was comfortable with soft dollars, the practice came under scrutiny from the federal government as part of the ERISA legislation of 1974. This caused a major upheaval in our fledgling industry. Firms had to rethink their business models; O'Brien Associates split up, and Wilshire Associates formed, as a result. At Russell, we moved away from soft dollars for a year or two, until the legislative intent became clearer.[3]

Even today, soft-dollar compensation remains controversial, though I don't see why. The real issue is disclosure. If all parties understand the costs, the benefits can be substantial. It's another example of the market working—with far more insight than the regulators.

Top 40 Hits: 1970–1974

Once we figured out the basic model for pension fund consulting, I decided to attract a group of 40 corporate pension funds, which would be the core of our new business. I started the process, basically cold calling large companies around the United States. I did have one major advantage: Throughout the period from the beginning of 1970 through about the middle of 1974, I was the only peddler doing this. I would go on trips about every other week. Sometimes I'd extend that to a week and a half between trips, as the agenda was always pretty busy. I'd try to visit companies in five different cities, with an average of five meetings per day, or 25 meetings for the five-day trip. And, by the middle of 1974, Frank Russell Company had 40 consulting clients, including AT&T and Xerox, which were among the largest corporate pension funds in the world at that time.

I picked the number *40* out of the air. I made a rough estimate of assets and revenues, and then made a guess that 40 would be a good number. I did not want to have an unlimited client list because I knew that it would become an overriding difficulty to handle.

I figured that if we had 40 of the top companies, we would be a five-star type of operation. And by setting a target of 40, we would all know where we were heading. When we went from number 25 to 26, we knew that there were only 14 more to go. It helped us internally to have a specific goal.

The clients liked it as well, because they figured that with a limited number of other accounts, they'd be maximizing the intelligence assets that they would get from us: They would get a personal, hands-on relationship, which ended up being a critically important part of the equation in terms of building up trust and setting expectations. Frank Russell Company clients knew that if they brought an idea or problem to us, we'd listen very attentively.

27

Minimal Debt; Reinvest

The final point I want to raise in this chapter has nothing to do with cold calls, but does reflect a patient, persistent approach to business. I'm referring to my reluctance to take on debt. In fact, I did it only twice while building the company.

The first time happened right after we confirmed our engagement with JCPenney. My father George was still the owner, even though he had nothing to do with the day-to-day operations of Frank Russell Company. I think he was still disappointed that I hadn't come to work for him. It was obvious that I needed to have an interest in the business, and my dad and I got into serious and, often, difficult discussions about it. He eventually decided *not* to sell me the company. Finally, some of his friends confronted him. They told him, "Look, sell the company to your son and forget it." Their influence brought him around and, using lawyers, we arrived at a price in the neighborhood of $250,000 for a company that had very small revenues and no more than $20,000 in the bank. It was overpriced, but I wanted to get rid of the problem. Also, my dad wanted a single lump-sum payment, so I had to borrow the money. Fortunately, I met two senior vice presidents at the National Bank of Washington who liked what I was doing. They thought it was risky, but interesting. As it turned out, things went well enough that I was able to pay them back within a 12-month period.

The second time I borrowed money was several years later, when, for regulatory reasons, I needed to buy a seat on the New York Stock Exchange. I paid a record price as I recall and had to get a loan as a result. I also repaid that one as quickly as possible.

Was this a visionary or an evolutionary approach? Definitely the latter. I had no picture of what Frank Russell Company would look like 10 years, 20 years, 30 years later—none at all. Even in hindsight, all I can say is, it takes a lot to build a business. If you don't have a clear vision for the next Amazon.com, the best you can do is allow the business to grow and become profitable. In any growth business you have to plow back your profits into the company so you can afford to hire smart, capable people who will help you grow at an even faster rate. That's a key point, which I'll discuss in detail in the next chapter.

So, when you talk about vision and evolution, evolution definitely wins hands-down, at least in my experience. I know that some people say I was a visionary, but honestly, in 1970 all I was thinking was, "Let's try to get 40 clients over the next four years." You could call that a four-year vision if you want to. But I'd say that's developing a business plan after a couple of lucky breaks.

Notes

1. Michael J. Clowes, *The Money Flood* (New York: John Wiley & Sons, 2000).
2. Ibid.
3. Ibid.

Key Points from Chapter 2

1. Stay busy. Activity will take you places you can't predict and a great idea can evolve where it's least expected.
2. It takes time to build a business and a little boredom along the way can be a good sign. When you're bored it means you're ready for something new. Stay alert and make it happen.
3. Don't overlook sales skills. It's rare that a product or service is in such demand that it "sells itself." Cold calling may seem repugnant (and it is difficult), but if you learn how to do it, you'll put yourself at a tremendous advantage.
4. Once you get your lucky break and make a big sale, that's only the beginning. How will you get paid? How will you provide the service? How can you make yourself indispensable over the long haul?
5. Avoid debt if you possibly can and continue to plow back the profits. It's the old-fashioned way, but it works.

CHAPTER

Hire People Smarter
Than You Are

"IT'S THE BEST INVESTMENT
YOU'LL EVER MAKE."

In the beginning, the entrepreneur is alone. You incubate your idea and personally handle all of the roles and responsibilities—whether it's R&D, sales, balancing the checkbook, or washing windows.

If you are successful, if your idea gains a foothold, then you will have the opportunity to hire people to help you. Generally, these will be people with specialized skills—a CFO, a sales professional, or a client executive. (I recommend you continue washing windows yourself; it sets a good example.)

This is an exciting time. If you can afford to increase headcount, you know you're doing well. And it's a relief to hand off some of the responsibilities. But it's also a critical time, a major inflection point that can have a long-lasting impact on the health of your organization. You can see this for yourself by using your index finger as a fulcrum for balancing a pencil.

First, point the tip of the pencil downwards if you are thinking of hiring people who will be subordinates. That's to say, if you plan to hire from a pool of people who are competent at performing a function, but who cannot be expected to excel in terms of intelligence or creativity.

Next, you should point the pencil upwards if you are thinking of hiring people who are more talented, creative, or intelligent than you are. This is a pool of people who may be brilliant specialists, already established in their field, or younger folks with a lot of smarts and drive, to the extent that they could easily surpass you if they fulfill their potential.

Now here's the payoff: The direction the pencil is pointing is an indicator of the future growth prospects of your enterprise. That's why it was always a fundamental precept for managers at Frank Russell Company—at every level of the organization—to "hire people smarter than you are."

The Need for Innovation in Pension Fund Management

Hiring smart people was imperative in the early years of Frank Russell Company. You have to keep in mind the challenges we faced. In the first place, there was not universal access to virtually unlimited computing power as there is today. To run any type of data-intensive study, you had to rent time from some large institution that had excess capacity, such as NASA.

As a result, some important breakthroughs from the academic world were not applied in a business setting in a timely way. Harry Markowitz published his thesis, "Portfolio Selection," in 1952.[1] Markowitz's work formed the basis for Modern Portfolio Theory, which laid out all of the principles of managing risk through diversification. However, without easy availability of computers—and data to put into the model—no one had developed a workable approach to asset allocation. So that was one of the challenges we had to overcome in the early 1970s.

Similarly, Peter Dietz's thesis, *Pension Funds: Measuring Investment Performance*, was published in 1966.[2] In his typically enterprising fashion, Peter managed to get his hands on several sets of historical data from a number of large trust banks. He put them to good use in constructing a method that enables pension funds to calculate managers' performance objectively. It was precisely the tool we needed as the basis for our manager comparisons. But in the early 1970s, the market had not picked up on "The Dietz Method," so that was an opportunity we were able to exploit.

In the next few pages, I'm going to tell the story of why and how I hired Peter Dietz and several other exceptionally smart people who were key to the development of Frank Russell Company's intellectual capital.

Peter Dietz and His Method of Performance Measurement

It wasn't long after JCPenney became a client that I got a telephone call from the chief financial officer at Penn Central Railroad. This was in September 1970. He said that the company had just gone bankrupt and they were having problems trying to figure out what to do with their pension account. He had heard about Frank Russell Company's pension consulting capabilities—we were the only one in the world at that time—and he invited me to come talk to them.

I flew to Philadelphia and had a good hour-and-a-half conversation with their senior people. Just as we were winding things up, they said, "Let's talk about performance measurement. How are you going to do that?"

At that time, I hadn't given much thought to performance measurement. I suppose that was on a middle burner; our number-one priority was picking good managers. However, by another stroke of good luck I had happened to hear, only a month or two before, about a man by the name of Peter Dietz who had developed an innovative formula for measuring pension performance. I didn't know all of the details, but I had a strong sense that it could work for our clients. With that in mind, I let my gut instinct take over and I heard myself saying, "Well, we use the Dietz Method, don't you?"

They hired us on the spot. That was on a Friday. I knew I had to get in touch with Peter Dietz right away. I came home on Saturday and found out that Peter had been at Columbia when he'd published his thesis on performance measurement and had then taken a job at Northwestern University. I called Northwestern and found out he was now working just down the road from us at the University of Oregon. Fortunately, I was able to get him on the phone, even though it was a Saturday, and persuaded him to drive up and talk to us the very next day.

As a professor, I think Peter was intrigued by the opportunity to step into the private sector. Our company was literally the only organization in the world that was in a position to put his knowledge to practical use. And that, apparently, was pretty exciting to him. By November, he agreed to work with us on a retainer basis.

Peter's input was critical to our work with Penn Central Railroad. Quoting from his *Pension Funds: Measuring Investment Performance*:

> Most pension plans are based on valuations made on original cost. They ignore unrealized appreciation, and take realized gains into the rate of return over an extended period [of] time. Others, such as that of Bethlehem Steel Corporation, use realized gains as an immediate reduction in necessary contributions. A few, such as that of Standard Oil of New Jersey, evaluate pension trust assets at market. These various methods can make substantial differences in corporate earnings, tax payments, and stock prices. A uniform method for measuring investment performance will aid in solving some of these conflicts.[3]

You can see why a proper valuation of the returns on the assets in the pension plan would be a major concern for various stakeholders of a company in bankruptcy.

But the Dietz Method was also an important tool in our day-to-day business of selecting managers. Historical performance was one of several key inputs in our selection process. But we needed to make sure we were comparing apples to apples.

For us to make a manager recommendation with full confidence, we had to be able to compare performance in different accounts on an objective basis. Similarly, we had to give sound data to our clients, so the chief financial officer could go to his board and extol the fund's performance—if it was good—in a way that would stand up against the inevitable questions and critiques.

At first, Peter provided his performance measurement service on a part-time basis. By March 1976, our demands on his time grew so great that we were able to entice him to join the company on a full-time basis. He was an important hire as, by that time, we did have some competition. It was a competitive advantage to be able to say we had the inventor of the Dietz Method on staff.

Over the next decade and a half, Peter filled many important roles at Russell. He performed some of our earliest manager research outside the United States, when he was in Europe in 1972. As director of research, he hired many of our leading innovators, including academics as well as people from the business community. Peter opened our Tokyo office in 1986, spearheading our effort to expand our intellectual capital in Asia. He was also one of the founders of the Q Group, otherwise known as the Institute for Quantitative Research in Finance.

Peter has been recognized throughout the industry as the pioneer of performance measurement. Within Frank Russell Company he was known as an open-minded colleague and a team player. It is interesting that Peter's actual performance measurement formula is fairly simple arithmetic. What distinguished it as a breakthrough insight was the clarity of thought it took to define the problem correctly, so the solution that Peter presented appeared to be simple and elegant. He encouraged a similar clarity of thought in colleagues and was always willing to change his mind—provided you could present your case convincingly.

Tragically, Peter suffered an untimely death in 1990; this was a great loss and he is still sorely missed by all of us.

Helane Grill, Madelyn Smith, and Joan Sobba—The Three Musketeers of Manager Research

Thanks to our association with Peter Dietz, Frank Russell Company was able to compare the performance of managers and funds. However, I was convinced right from the beginning that performance alone wouldn't tell the whole story.

In 1969, the concept of the investment boutique was already starting to take hold. Talented portfolio managers with an entrepreneurial bent were leaving the big institutions to start their own shops. Between the trust banks and insurance companies, mutual funds, and the new investment boutiques, we had a full plate. I needed to focus on filling out my client roster and serving existing clients. That's why I decided to start hiring and training people who would specialize in evaluating investment managers.

My first hire came recommended by a Harvard classmate. I met Helane Grill on a street corner on Wall Street and offered her a job the same afternoon.

Helane had a tough job. Other than the 20 or so managers I had researched for JCPenney, she had the rest of the universe to tackle. We had very few guidelines to give her—nobody had ever had the job of *manager research analyst* before. And she had to work by herself in New York City.

In fact, we couldn't afford to rent proper office space for Helane. A friend who worked at C. J. Lawrence, which was housed in one of the older buildings in lower Manhattan, loaned us a space in the attic that had been used to store furniture. It really was nothing more than a closet. Over the years, the two facts— that I met Helane on a street corner and her office had been a closet—have blended together and become part of the company's lore: *Helane Grill worked out of a phone booth.*

If that conjures up an image of Superman—or Superwoman— then it's all to the good. Helane had all the qualities needed to set the definitive standard for manager research: She was, and is, intelligent, articulate, and motivated. To get her started, we had a role-playing session. My experience as a portfolio manager at Bondstock had helped me develop the questions I'd asked the managers on Paul Kaltinick's list. I used those questions to interview myself, playing both the role of the researcher and the portfolio manager. Helane wrote it all down and used that as her Bible, at least for the first few interviews. She decided to start with a portfolio manager she'd happened to meet at a cocktail party. His firm ran just a few mutual funds, and she was already acquainted with him, so she felt he'd be a suitable guinea pig. And that's all it took to get her up and running.

Not long after Helane started, we had a client whose trust agreement required them to use a bank to manage their pension assets. They gave us a list of 100 banks they wanted us to research. Helane took on this project, calling the banks to get their performance data.

Everybody asks Helane if it was tough at first to get a foot in the door at places like J.P. Morgan. Her answer usually comes as a surprise: In general, the money managers were polite and often quite gracious.

Of course, the people Helane was interviewing were almost exclusively male, while she was an elegant young woman dressed in nicely tailored black or white linen suits, depending on the season. When you think about it, those poor money managers really were overmatched. Here's how Helane describes it:

> There's no question that the different sexes played a role. I'm a girl from the right side of the tracks in Boston. I dressed the part and I spoke the part. I knew the money managers would much rather look at me in my pearls—because Boston girls wore pearls—than at a man doing the same job. I didn't flirt; I was just being a woman in a male-dominated profession and I felt I had every right to use every talent I had to get my job done.

Inevitably, there were a few people who tried to dodge Helane's requests for an interview. They might succeed in putting her off a time or two. Eventually, in every case she got the interview. She was as tenacious as a bulldog—which is to say that she was *almost* as tenacious as Dick Lothrop.

Over the years, our operation became more mature and we hired dozens of additional manager research analysts. Among her peers, Helane has the reputation of being the best ever at developing a rapport with managers—a skill that enabled her to ferret out the essential truths about their operations, investment process, personnel issues, and so on. She truly set the standard for qualitative manager research.

After Helane, the next person I hired was Madelyn Smith. She joined Frank Russell Company in February 1971. Madelyn had an accounting background, so we started her out assisting Peter Dietz in performance measurement. She sat directly outside my office, where I often had her listen in on conversations with clients. By April, we felt Madelyn was ready to start meeting managers in person. She joined Helane in Dallas for a series of interviews. As it turned out, the two formed an immediate friendship, which lasts to this day. After that trip, Madelyn assumed responsibility for managers in the western states, while Helane covered the east.

Madelyn proved to be tenacious as well. On her first trip to New York City, she was taking a taxi from the airport. There was a problem with the car; I think the drive shaft fell off and the taxi collided with the concrete divider, caromed across the highway and ended up on its side in a ditch. Fortunately, Madelyn and the driver were both uninjured. The man helped her crawl out of the window, and then assumed they would both wait there for the police to show up. Madelyn would have none of that: Helane was expecting her and they had work to do.

She flagged down a bus, but the occupants spoke only Spanish. Although Madelyn had no idea where they were heading, she got on anyway. Fortunately, they dropped her off at Madison Square Garden about a half-hour later. By then, Madelyn was ready to risk another cab ride. A gentleman saw her and offered to help carry her luggage to the taxi stand. Madelyn accepted, and a few minutes later she was safe and sound in Helane's apartment. But when Madelyn told the story of her adventure, Helane seemed to ignore the taxi flipping over; what upset her was the fact that Madelyn had let a stranger carry her luggage!

About six months after Madelyn joined the company, I hired Joan Sobba as my executive assistant. Joan had a lot of experience, holding a variety of positions both in state government and with several different businesses. In fact, she had *too much* experience, having changed jobs, almost like clockwork, every two years. I could see she was energetic, a real go-getter—and that she'd be a great assistant, provided she'd be willing to stay on the job for a while. I offered her the position on the condition that she'd give me a minimum of three years. She agreed—reluctantly—but ended up staying for over 30, in increasingly responsible roles.

In the early days, Joan did some manager research, but quickly realized that she preferred working on the business side of the company. She gravitated to an administrative role and became the glue that held our manager research operation together. Joan and Madelyn sat at adjacent desks and stayed in close contact with Helane by telephone. I called them the "Three Musketeers" because I knew they were intrepid and capable, and I could always depend on them to get the job done. In hiring them, we raised the level of competence at Frank Russell Company; in turn, their work transformed the industry in ways that few people fully realize.

Creating a Universe

While Helane was busy gathering data on banks' performance at our clients' request, I gave Madelyn an additional list that I thought would be of interest. In the end we had a collection of approximately 175 banks. As we collected the data, we would send it down to Peter Dietz, who was still at the University of Oregon. Peter would formulate the risk and return numbers and send it back to us.

Then we had the idea—I think Madelyn and I came up with the same thought independently—to chart banks' performance on a grid, with risk and return as the two axes. Joan would execute the charts by hand and add the dots with a typewriter. This was the first use of a scatter diagram to depict a universe of managers.

The analysis of the scatter diagrams gave further support to our thesis: The fact that trust banks were doing a subpar job of managing money validated our premise that managers should be hired based on demonstrated skill—not on relationships or reputation. We also gained some important insight into the practice of "balanced management," which was common at that time. A balanced manager had discretion to invest all of its clients' assets. The banks employing the balanced approach typically claimed that they were adding value through their ability to adjust the percentages of stocks and bonds in the portfolio to take advantage of market conditions. Our research showed that in most cases they were changing the allocation by a mere five percent, one way or the other. A change this small had no meaningful impact on return or risk. And more often than not they got the timing wrong.

A New Process for a New Industry

The organization was growing. We now had several executives focused on clients in addition to myself. Madelyn and Helane focused on equities, Don Hardy researched fixed income, Blake Eagle was in charge of real estate, and Joan kept everybody together and all of our projects on track.

To create high-quality work that exceeded client expectations, we needed a disciplined process. It's interesting to look back and see how our business process functioned in the days before personal computers.

After I would sign up a new client, we would have extensive conversations so I could learn about the current status of the pension fund. I would write a detailed report of everything I'd learned and send it back to the client, both to confirm that I had an accurate understanding and to suggest the next steps. A copy of this document would go into our file.

Meanwhile, all of our researchers—Madelyn, Helane, Don, and Blake—were documenting their manager visits. Copies of their observations plus the supporting data also went into our central filing system. And when our other consultants met with clients, their notes would go into the files as well.

We called the service we were offering *capital placement*. In essence, we were advising pension funds on which firms to choose to invest their assets. After passage of the Employee Income Retirement Security Act of 1974 (ERISA), pension funds also needed documentation that showed they had made prudent, responsible decisions based on professional expertise. To meet these needs, we created a document called "the strategy report," or simply, "the strategy." If we were analyzing the status of merely a single manager, for example, the report could be relatively short—a dozen or so pages. If we were reviewing the structure of an entire pension fund, the strategy could be quite lengthy. For example, the comprehensive report we delivered to General Motors in 1983 filled five large notebooks. That's how I remember it. Again, company lore has transmuted this to a stack of paper *five feet high*. (I doubt a report of that magnitude would have exceeded GM's expectations for quality.)

To produce our recommended list of managers, we had to analyze both qualitative and quantitative data and arrive at a consensus. Thus, the whole team met frequently—Helane participated via telephone—to discuss the pros and cons of each firm. Smart people are also rather argumentative and, I can tell you, we had some good discussions. That was part of our culture; everybody felt free to speak their minds and it wasn't a problem.

We also had an annual seminar, which everyone would attend in person. This was a forum for our annual review of managers, client strategies, and miscellaneous issues that required immediate attention. Joan took charge of coordinating the seminars and, of course, we documented everything in writing.

When it came time to submit a strategy report, Joan would get the ball rolling. She would pull together and distill the information from all of the notes, data, and strategy discussions into a first draft. Next, the team would get to work and edit the report.

Remember, there was no word processing, so every version had to be typed by hand. It was the same for charts and tables—there were no automated spreadsheets with 3-D graphics capabilities. Everything had to be done precisely by hand with rulers and indelible ink. It was a lot of work.

Finally, I'd deliver the report in person, perhaps with another member of the team. We'd have discussions with the client and, of course, document the key points in preparation for the next report.

Madelyn Smith Shows Her Style

By the mid-1970s, we had already developed a good qualitative sense of how to determine which managers had skill. We knew diversification was important, but we didn't have the tools to optimize the manager mix. And we hadn't been through a complete investment cycle.

At first, we thought past performance would be a good quantitative indicator. It seemed reasonable to assume that a manager who had had the skill to do well in the past ought to be able to continue to do well in the future. Empirical results quickly showed that this was not the case.

Next, we looked deeply into Bill Sharpe's Capital Asset Pricing Model and developed the notion that beta might be our holy grail. Then came the ferocious bear market of 1973–1974. *Beta* is a measure of variability relative to the Index. High-beta stocks should do much better than the Index in up markets, and much worse during downturns. The same should hold true for managers who hold a lot of high-beta stocks. As expected, the high-beta managers got hammered by the recession. But then, in 1975, when the market began to recover, the high-beta contingent didn't lead the charge the way they were supposed to. That prompted Madelyn to take another look.

I'm going to let "the mother of equity styles" tell the rest of the story in her own words:

> I thought there was something going on that we were missing
> and capital market theory wasn't helping us at all. We hired

an analyst to do statistics on portfolios. I wanted to know things like dividend yield, P/E ratio, and return on equity. We ended up with ten basic factors in addition to performance. This was our first equity profile.

We knew that when the market turned, the high-yield, low P/E managers had gone up the most, even though, theoretically, they weren't supposed to because they were low-beta managers. So, we visited them and found out how different they were philosophically from high-beta stock managers, and our equity profile confirmed that the two groups had different equity characteristics.

The next step was figuring out how to characterize the two groups. Thanks to Graham and Dodd's influential book, *Security Analysis,*[4] the terms *value* and *growth* had been widely used since at least the 1930s. But these terms were used only to refer to different stocks, never to portfolios. Madelyn's insight was that each manager's *philosophy* led him to invest almost exclusively in either growth or value stocks. So, she extended the terms *growth* and *value* to managers, with precise definitions of the philosophical approaches and portfolio characteristics of each style.

Our identification of equity styles gave us an important new tool for diversifying risk within the equity portion of the portfolio. Dun & Bradstreet in 1975 was the first pension fund in which we implemented a rudimentary style-balanced portfolio. Then in 1978, another client did a major revamp based on the concept of style diversification.

Today, style diversification is widely used throughout the industry. However, the first clients using it had to accept the idea that approximately half of their equities would be underperforming at any given time. Of course, they would be compensated by always having holdings in the style that the market favored.

Russ Fogler—Pioneer of Asset Allocation

The year 1974 was a watershed for Frank Russell Company because of the passage of ERISA. I mentioned it briefly in the previous section, but ERISA deserves a bit more explanation because it plays such a major role in our industry. ERISA put the concept of fiduciary responsibility front and center. Plan sponsors were now legally responsible for acting prudently, in the sole interest of participants. In order to act prudently, pension funds needed the appropriate investment expertise and, if the fund did not possess that expertise internally, ERISA mandated that the fiduciary hire someone with the professional knowledge to properly implement the investment and other functions.

As you read this summary, I won't blame you if you assume that we must have lobbied Congress to write legislation specifically tailored to promote the interests of pension fund consultants. A lucky coincidence? Remember, by 1974 we already had a full roster of 40 clients. In essence, you could say that ERISA marked the moment when the government started to catch up to the market.

ERISA didn't benefit us financially, but it did spur us to think more systematically about what it meant to be prudent. Clearly, we needed to do everything we could to measure and manage risk. And to do that, we needed a workable asset allocation system.

That's why Peter Dietz called Russ Fogler in March 1975. Russ had earned his Ph.D. at Columbia under Roger Murray, who was also Peter's mentor. Then Russ spent a few years at a military think tank where he developed world-class programming skills while working on some of the most powerful computers available at the time. That's what prompted Peter's call.

In 1975, Russ had a teaching position at the University of Florida, but he was hungry for part-time consulting work. As Russ likes to say, "For an academic, access to data and a real-world problem to solve is like sex." He knew that Russell had voluminous data from our clients, and a pretty exciting problem. That spring, back in Gainesville, he got right to work.

Harry Markowitz published "Portfolio Selection" in 1952, so the principles of diversification and identifying the efficient frontier had been understood for quite some time. The problem was implementing that knowledge, because the essential inputs to the model did not exist. Looking back, it's hard to believe, but something as elemental as historical returns from stocks and bonds was not generally available. That became Russ's first challenge: to assemble a workable data series of asset class performance.

Without going into all the technical details, he started with the data compiled by Standard & Poor's, beginning in 1926. And he spliced that together with another set of data from the Cowles Foundation, dating back to the 1800s. Russ likes round numbers, so he chose 1900 as the start date. Little did he know that Roger Ibbotson and Rex Sinquefield were working on the same problem at the same time. They published their study in 1976, using S&P's data for the 1926–1974 period.

Once he had the data he needed, Russ sat down to design a model. He decided to take a different approach than the standard Markowitz matrix, which graphs returns on one axis and standard deviation on the other. Russ felt that people don't think in terms of standard deviation. Instead, he created a model built on curves that showed the probability of being underfunded with different asset mixes. He also added a third dimension that represented the pension fund's required rate of return.

Russ returned to Tacoma in June with his stack of 80-column punch cards that contained the new asset allocation model. Now Russ is actually a very down-to-earth person. He *pooh-poohs* the notion that what we do in the investment business is rocket science; to him, it's all common sense. We had our top consultants in the room, and we also invited Jim Curtis, who was a highly respected actuary from Milliman and Robertson, based just up I-5 in Seattle. We asked Russ to present his concept to all of us, including Jim, as though we were clients. Russ is not shy, so he was happy to do it:

> So I get up there with my Ph.D. mentality and I explained the whole thing. I remember being pretty proud of it. I turned to Jim and said, "What do you think?" And Jim replied, "I don't really understand what you're talking about."

Now, I'm not so stupid that I didn't realize I had one of the smartest people in the pension funds industry here. He was an actuary, which meant he was mathematical. In short, when someone like Jim Curtis tells me he doesn't understand what I'm talking about, it's a pretty clear sign that I'm the one with the problem—not him.

After Jim left, Russ went over to Peter Dietz. He apologized for what happened and swore he'd be able to fix it if he could just sit down at a computer terminal. Peter gave him access to our account and Russ stayed up into the wee hours, reprogramming the model. He simplified the third dimension, and we invited Jim Curtis to come back from Seattle the next day. Russ showed him the revised model and, this time, Jim responded enthusiastically.

Now we had our asset allocation model, though we still had to introduce it to clients. I think Russ was a little hesitant to do that right away, because we'd only tested it internally. However, I felt sure it was ready to go. I convinced Russ to come along with us and, over the next two weeks, we demonstrated our asset allocation model to 19 clients in several different cities. It was quite a trip. Russ's model was a breakthrough for us and gave us a competitive advantage for quite a few years.

Russ continued to do project work for Russell every summer for approximately 10 years. Working with Don Hardy and Peter Dietz, he created a bond model that finally gave us an objective way to evaluate bond managers' performance. Another important project was the work he did on equity styles with Madelyn Smith. After Madelyn had created her style classification, we wanted to test it quantitatively. Russ used cluster diagrams to analyze managers' characteristics. The result was gratifying: The quantitative test confirmed that our existing methodology was right on the money.

Duncan Smith Asks the Tough Questions—and Answers Them

Every entrepreneur needs someone like Duncan Smith. You need a gadfly, an iconoclast, a contrarian, who is passionate about the company and isn't afraid to speak his mind. If you can find one as insightful as Duncan Smith, you'll have a business asset whose value can never be underestimated.

Duncan Smith grew up in Texas and trained as a mechanical engineer. Early in his career he worked at Texas Instruments, but found that his expenses were growing at a higher rate than his salary. He solved that problem by learning how to make money in the stock market. A career change followed and, before too long, he found himself in New York City heading up the national marketing effort for a Merrill Lynch subsidiary called Lionel D. Edie. Then he moved to Peat Marwick as head of the pension practice. But the culture of an accounting firm left him feeling restless. Somehow, Peter Dietz heard about Duncan's availability, and the next thing I knew, he appeared in my office at 7:30 one morning. Duncan was at least two hours early for his interview with Peter. And with his pipe, cowboy boots, and western-cut jacket, he looked as much like Wild Bill Hickok as he did a pension fund consultant.

But after speaking with him for 45 minutes, I was ready to hire him. Duncan knew what he was talking about and he was a straight shooter. I liked him immediately. So did our consulting clients. He had quite an affinity for companies in heavy industries such as energy and manufacturing, perhaps because of his engineering background. In any case, he became the executive in charge of relationships with companies such as Shell, British Petroleum, Sun, Hercules, General Motors, and Xerox.

Not long after Duncan joined the company, we had a report due for General Motors. It was an important document, outlining our strategic recommendations. For some reason, preparation of the report fell behind schedule and we drafted Duncan to complete it as he said he had worked on similar projects at Peat Marwick.

True to his word, Duncan got the report ready in time. But when I reviewed the draft, I saw some recommendations that I was not expecting. I didn't think they would fly with GM's management, and I asked Joan Sobba to convene an emergency meeting to see whether we could pull together another draft in time.

There was no time to properly notify Duncan or to give him the opportunity to make revisions. When he heard about my decision, he was upset. That's putting it mildly. He came charging into my office and asked me point blank why I had nixed his draft.

I explained to him that he had taken the day-to-day decision-making authority in the pension plan away from the committee of the board that had always been responsible for it. In fact, at General Motors everything was run by committees of the board, and had been since the 1930s, when DuPont bailed out GM. DuPont was also run by committees of the board, so the practice was deeply ingrained in GM's culture. Although Duncan's plan made sense, I didn't think GM would ever accept such a major departure from their management practices.

But Duncan was not about to give up so easily. "Wouldn't it be more practical? Isn't it the right thing to do?"

That got me. As you know, I'm a great believer in doing the right thing.

"If they reject this proposal," Duncan persisted, "at least we'll know that we gave our best advice, and it will be documented. And if they accept it"—I cut him off. He had won the argument. I agreed to submit his recommendation, but I thought Duncan was dreaming to suppose that GM might actually go for it.

In any event, that's exactly what happened. GM accepted our streamlined decision-making structure. It was the first area in GM to get away from management at the board level. That innovation soon spread to other departments in GM. And it was all because Duncan Smith had the confidence to tell me what I needed to hear.

Duncan's experience in running portfolios simultaneously for individual and institutional accounts gave him unique insights that benefited all of our clients. In any organization there has to be a trade-off between teamwork and the ability to make decisions in a timely way. I'll talk about this in detail in Chapter 7, "Recognize Luck."

At Frank Russell Company, we encouraged open discussion with the idea that airing conflicting opinions could lead to consensus. Of course, Duncan loathed committee decision making.

He understood the necessity for extended discussion when it came to long-term, strategic business issues. But he felt it was madness to try to run money that way.

That's why I put him in a chief investment officer role for our funds for several years when we wanted to improve our performance. Duncan stepped in, and the first thing he did was fire a value manager that had outperformed the S&P 500 every year. Sounds counterintuitive, doesn't it?

Duncan realized that the manager typically held half of its assets in cash. That helped in years when value was underperforming and allowed the manager to beat the index. But the cash position created a mismatch with the value index, which was a serious problem for us. In a style-diversified fund it is important that the managers' processes be a true reflection of their benchmarks. This particular manager was not willing to run a fully invested portfolio, so Duncan felt we had no choice but to terminate it.

As Duncan puts it, "A committee could never have made the decision to fire a manager that outperformed the S&P 500 every year. You have to give somebody the authority to select managers and make them accountable for the performance of the fund."

During his tenure, Duncan helped make our Equity I Fund a top-quartile performer. More importantly, he showed all of us the importance of having a single person accountable for each fund's performance. He recognized that institutions have an infinite time horizon only in theory; in practice, they are run by human beings who demand competitive short-term results.

Although he retired from Frank Russell Company several years ago, Duncan's clients simply won't let him stop working. He continues to consult to a select few, and I depend on his expertise to guide the investment strategy at Threshold Group and The Russell Family Foundation.

Don Ezra Defines the Right Way to Be a Fiduciary

Don Ezra was the first actuary to work at Frank Russell Company. We hired him in 1984, and it's interesting to reflect that we managed to advise defined benefit (DB) plans for 15 years without an actuary on staff. In those days, our job was to focus on the investment side of the equation, leaving the clients to calculate their liabilities. They would tell us their required rate of return and we would provide the investment strategy that would get them there most efficiently.

Don changed all that—but not right away. His initial responsibility was to open our office in Toronto and establish Russell's consulting practice in Canada. By 1989, we fully understood what a valuable asset we had and we brought him back to Tacoma to head asset allocation research. That was the year I gave up the title of president, handing the reins to Mike Phillips. We needed someone to take over Mike's role as head of consulting, and Don was the logical choice.

Now we had somebody who could talk to the clients about their assumptions, and challenge their actuaries in his charming, yet penetrating way. Don developed Russell's asset/liability model, which finally allowed us to look at both sides of the equation.

In my view, that was, and continues to be, Don's major contribution to Russell—not the asset/liability model per se, but the kind of thinking it represents. Don is a big picture thinker, but he'd be the first to warn you that he is not an innovator. He calls himself a *synthesizer*, but I'm not sure if that's quite right either. His unique skill is to spot the incoming blips on the horizon, and identify which ones are important ideas and which are safe to ignore. Then he subjects the important ones to rigorous analysis from every conceivable perspective.

We recognized that Don's mindset was a valuable complement to that of Duncan Smith. Whereas Duncan was the company gadfly, scrutinizing every detail *within* the organization, Don was our spotter, an advance scout with an eagle eye scanning in every direction. For a while, we combined their considerable talents, along with those of Ernie Bianco, who had been our head of consulting, into an informal advisory body that we called our "top-down group."

Their mission was simply to take a macro perspective on the economy, markets, the industry, and our position in it. We wanted them to challenge each other and report back on the results.

This is one of my convictions about managing smart people: It's always a good idea to put them together and allow the synergies to develop.

However, as is often the case with senior people, management responsibilities interfere and it's hard to find the time to follow through with your best ideas. That was the case with Duncan, when he decided his real love was working directly with clients. Don had a similar feeling. Although his position as director of consulting gave him a seat on the board and made him one of the most responsible and influential people in the company, he preferred to step away from that role. He made the case quite simply and persuasively: He would add more value by doing what he loved best.

We created a new role for him: *director of strategic advice.* Here's what Don had to say about his "demotion":

> I can't tell you what a joy it is to work at a company where the culture is to hire good people, whether you have an explicit role for them or not, and let them do what they need to do. I had been one of the top people in the company and then decided I didn't want to continue down that path. I like the notion of ideas and making things happen with clients, rather than running things internally. For me it's fantastic to find myself in a position where someone like me can continue to have an influence that has nothing to do with hierarchical rank.

I cite this as evidence that *autonomy* can be a more effective management tool than promotions and power, if your goal is to retain and properly utilize top senior talent.

Over the years, Don put his autonomy to good use. When issues would crop up as hot topics, Don was generally at or ahead of the curve with timely analysis. He researched the likely consequences resulting from the underfunding of the U.S. Social Security system, and analyzed the costs and benefits of competing plans to address the situation. For pension plans, he led the way in evaluating alternative approaches to risk control, including risk budgeting and Value at Risk. For those in the brave new 401(k) world, he articulated lessons that sponsors of defined contribution (DC) plans could learn from decades of DB experience. Also in the DC space, he examined emerging concepts of behavioral finance and the management of longevity risk as people "decumulate" their wealth.

Finally, Don did important work in defining the responsibilities of fiduciaries and best practices for pension fund governance. I'd like to comment on this point in a bit more detail, as I believe this will prove to be Don's most lasting achievement. Don's key insight is that there is often a disconnect between the Pension Committee that has ultimate responsibility for the fund's success and the day-to-day investment management process. In essence, Duncan Smith was raising a version of this question when he recommended that General Motors avoid having every decision made by "committees of the board." All of our consultants ran up against this problem, as it was—and is—part of the industry's structure: While pension committees are composed of intelligent, experienced business-people, many of them have no formal training in the disciplines of investment management. In addition, they meet only quarterly, whereas markets can turn on a dime and issues with managers typically can't wait until the next board meeting for resolution.

It took Don's insightful and disciplined mind to analyze the proper roles and responsibilities for everyone involved in pension fund management. He described all of this in detail in the book he wrote with co-author Keith Ambachtsheer, *Pension Fund Excellence*.[5] It is essential reading for anyone involved with institutional investing. But I also recommend it to businesspeople in any industry as a classic demonstration of the right way to think about governance and the proper delegation of decision-making responsibilities.

The Best Investment I Ever Made

The group of people I've just introduced—Peter Dietz, Madelyn Smith, Helane Grill, Joan Sobba, Russ Fogler, Duncan Smith, and Don Ezra—aren't the only smart people I hired over the years.

Blake Eagle pioneered the research of real estate managers; Don Hardy did some of the early work on fixed income and later spearheaded our research in alternative strategies. Both could have been included alongside the Three Musketeers.

Jan Twardowski initiated our international efforts, which now produce a significant percentage of the company's revenue.

Kelly Haughton invented the Russell Indexes that provide most of our name recognition.

And Andy Turner built our mind-bogglingly complex multi-period stochastic optimization model, which represents a major breakthrough in how we manage risk.

These are just a few of the extremely intelligent and capable people I have had the privilege of working with over the years. I simply had to find a way to limit the size of this chapter or it would have taken over the entire book. You will meet the others later, at the proper time and place.

The group I chose for this chapter happened to be instrumental in developing the intellectual capital that made us the preeminent pension fund consultant in the 1970s and early 1980s. Their work became the foundation of everything we accomplished, and that remains true today, in my opinion. This is why I believe that hiring people who are smarter than I am is the best investment I ever made.

Notes

1. Harry Markowitz, "Portfolio Selection," *The Journal of Finance*, Vol. 7, No. 1 (Mar., 1952), pp. 77–91.
2. Peter O. Dietz, "Pension Funds: Measuring Investment Performance" (master's thesis, New York Graduate School of Business, Columbia University and Free Press, 1966).
3. Peter O. Dietz, *Pension Funds: Measuring Investment Performance* (Somerset, NJ: TSG, The Spaulding Series, 2004), pp. 6–7.
4. Benjamin Graham and David L. Dodd, *Security Analysis* (New York: McGraw-Hill, 1934).
5. Keith P. Ambachtsheer and D. Don Ezra, *Pension Fund Excellence* (New York: John Wiley and Sons, 1998).

Key Points from Chapter 3

1. When hiring, always try to sustain an upward trend in the intelligence/skill level of the organization.
2. Hire exceptionally talented people, even if you don't have a specific role for them.
3. Synergy is important. Look for people with different thinking styles and skills and then encourage them to collaborate. The results can be surprising.
4. Give your people the leeway to explore. Dark alleys may lead to green pastures.

CHAPTER

Be Creative

"THE ONLY DIFFERENCE IS THE ZEROS."

When you hire smart people and give them autonomy, you can expect an explosion of creativity. We saw that in the last chapter. The key question for you as a business-person is how to transform all of your exciting, new intellectual capital into products and services that people will pay for. And that may require a certain amount of creativity on your part.

At Russell, our approach was incremental. Once we had developed a core competence, researching U.S. equity and fixed-income managers, we looked for ways to continue to add value for our clients. At first, that often meant extrapolating an exist-ing capability into new markets; later on, we found ways to lever-age our intellectual capital into new lines of business.

The Treasurer's Club: They're Not Laughing Anymore

As usual, this story begins with Paul Kaltinick. It was 1971, and we had been working together for about one year. Paul had recently joined The Treasurers Club in New York. As the youngest member, he became program chairman, with responsibility for recruiting speakers for their meetings. Paul asked me to present an overview of what we were doing to improve pension fund performance. He said that the audience usually consisted of about 40 treasurers from large corporations with headquarters in New York City. From a peddler's point of view, this was impossible to resist.

The theme of the speech was "the buck stops here." By 1971, people were waking up to the underfunded status of many large corporations' pension funds. I observed that it would no longer be possible for companies to lay the responsibility for funding shortfalls on their trustees: They were on the hook; they had to act, and the real question was, "What do we do now?"

I talked about objective setting, performance measurement, and using appropriate benchmarks. Familiar topics. I then moved on to the problem of manager selection, and I proposed that multiple management was a solution we favored—as long as you didn't overdo it. For example, I cited companies "that use 20 managers when their pension assets are only $200 million in size." Too bad we didn't have our commingled funds available; they would have done the job nicely.

This message resonated well with the treasurers. Then I came to the point where I observed that U.S. equities had not always led the way in performance:

> It disturbs me to recognize that in 1940 stocks yielded 8% and bonds were yielding 2%, yet most of the pension money was going into bonds. Today the situation is reversed. Stocks are yielding 2% and bonds are yielding 8%. And yet most of the pension assets are going into stocks. Doesn't that make you wonder about the effectiveness of U.S. common stocks in the next ten years? *Doesn't that raise the question as to whether we should be considering real estate and foreign stocks in the selection of our money managers?*

I went on to predict that, within 10 years, most pension funds would have significant allocations to these two new asset classes: real estate and international equities.

Here the response was much less positive. I don't think anyone laughed out loud, but I do remember a fair amount of skeptical chuckling. At the time, U.S. pension funds had no meaningful exposure to real estate or non-U.S. equities. Most people hadn't even considered the possibility. So it's not surprising that my audience was skeptical.

But we didn't let that stop us.

Blake Eagle Puts Real Estate on the Map

We tackled real estate first, only because the logistics were so much easier. We didn't have to cross any oceans for manager interviews. Of course, real estate presented some formidable challenges that are unique to the asset class. At the time, there really weren't any suitable vehicles for institutional investors. Real estate investment trusts (REITs) were available, but they were being managed as financing vehicles, charging high fees for lending to developers. In 1970, REITs had suffered one of their periodic blowups due to excess leverage—sound familiar? We were looking for vehicles that avoided lending to third-party property operators and focused instead on the actual ownership of properties.

That raised the problem of diversification. Office buildings are expensive but, unlike stocks, there was no established public market for valuing or trading shares in commercial real estate. We still felt the concept was sound. But we knew it would require a lot of work and creativity to prepare a strategy we could present to our clients.

That job fell to Blake Eagle. Dick Lothrop hired Blake in 1971 to develop real estate syndicates that we could market to our Bondstock shareholders. Both Dick and Blake stayed with Frank Russell Company after the Bondstock spinoff. As the bear market of 1973 began to claw back the value of investors' equity holdings, I felt the time was ripe to start talking about a different asset class. One afternoon, I handed Blake a plane ticket and a list of four appointments we had set up for the next week in New York City, and that's how our real estate consulting capability got off the ground.

One of the people Blake met on that first trip was Meyer Melnikoff, who was the chief actuary at Prudential and founded the first real estate pooled fund in 1970. It was called Prudential Property Investment Separate Account (PRISA). Meyer had heard me speak about the importance of diversification, and he later told Blake that our position as advocates of adding a real estate component to pension fund portfolios had been a big help in getting PRISA off the ground.

In fact, the relationship was of mutual benefit. As Blake points out,

> Before Frank Russell Company got involved, pension funds and the real estate world knew absolutely nothing about one another. Pension funds had huge pools of capital; real estate is capital intensive: It was inevitable that they would find each other. Frank Russell Company happened to be on the leading edge. It was our role to educate the real estate world about pension funds, and vice versa. Our challenge was to build the bridge between them.

Building that bridge took a lot of creativity on Blake's part. First, he was dealing with two different cultures that spoke different languages. For example, property developers and managers think in terms of a building's *capitalization rate.* Equity investors are more familiar with a stock's P/E or *price-to-earnings ratio.* In fact, these two terms are simply the reciprocal of one another, but the language reflects a different thought process about investing.

In addition, property people had a culture of secrecy that resulted from real estate's status as a private market. Unlike the equity markets, where the price of every trade is flashed instantly around the world on a real or virtual tickertape, the value of a building is not a matter of public record. In those days, the operators didn't feel it was in their interest to make this information available. They were looking to buy low and sell high, and they felt it was an advantage to keep their competitors from having good information. In fact, it was not unusual for developers to leak misinformation into the market.

We had to have a solid analysis to bring to our clients. Large insurance companies like Prudential and the Equitable had significant data on property prices from their decades of selling insurance and investing in mortgages. That's where our relationships with people like Meyer Melnikoff paid off, and a big part of Blake's contribution was his success in convincing the large insurance companies that they could trust us to use their data with discretion.

At the same time, we continued sending Blake on trips to interview real estate managers around the country. By the end of 1973, he'd researched about a dozen managers and had commenced writing the first case for real estate investing by pension funds. The report was ready to show to clients in the spring of 1974. It made the case from the perspective of Modern Portfolio Theory—that adding an uncorrelated asset class to the portfolio was the most effective way to lower the overall risk level. We knew that real estate's return pattern was quite different than that of equities; the fact that real estate was a physical asset, not a financial one, made it a particularly effective diversifier. In addition, real estate could also play an important role as a hedge against inflation.

The case for real estate proved to be of great interest to pension funds in the mid-1970s. Chevron was a particularly receptive client; in late 1976 or early 1977, they decided to commit 10 percent of their portfolio to real estate. We thanked them for their vote of confidence and were about to head for home. Almost as an afterthought, their CIO asked us how we planned to measure the performance of their real estate managers: What benchmark did we plan to use?

Blake replied, "We're working on it."

This was certainly a creative response, consistent with the Russell tradition: We had just committed ourselves to building a real estate index! It took five years, but in 1982, we began publishing the NCREIF Property Index (NPI). NCREIF stands for "National Council of Real Estate Investment Fiduciaries," and we spun off the index to them as an independent entity. It was the right thing to do. However, during the NPI's formative years, I'd call Blake and ask him, "How much have we spent so far on this index?" And Blake would answer, "You don't want to know."

In fact, Blake's creativity resulted in major financial rewards. But it was definitely a long-term investment, as I'll explain later in the chapter. In the meantime, let me give you a sense of the size of the opportunity that real estate represented: In 1982, when the NPI started out, it tracked 235 properties worth $0.5 billion. As of 2008, there were 6,000 properties worth more than $330 billion. That works out to a growth in assets of approximately 25 percent per year.

London Calling

It took a bit longer for our international capabilities to get off the ground. By chance, Peter Dietz was living in Belgium in 1972 while he was on sabbatical from the University of Oregon. We asked him to interview as many European managers as possible—while he was in the neighborhood. But that was just a foot in the door, rather than a systematic, sustained manager research program.

However, we continued to believe that the opportunity was compelling. Again, based on Modern Portfolio Theory, we argued that diversifying into international equities could reduce the overall portfolio's risk without sacrificing return.

It was 1979 when I felt we were finally ready to open a new office in London. I hired Jan Twardowski to run the new operation. Jan had started with Wellington and then was one of the founders of Vanguard along with John Bogle. Jan had previously represented Wellington in Paris, which, I felt, qualified him to introduce Frank Russell Company's services to Europe.

Not surprisingly, Jan wanted to know what his job description was. I told him simply, "Just do the same thing that we've already done in the U.S." Jan looked at me with a blank stare for a bit; he must have been expecting more explicit instructions. But I knew he was a go-getter and perfectly capable of taking a broad concept and executing it in a way that would prove to be productive.

It was a two-part strategy. First, we were encouraging our U.S. clients to put approximately 15 percent of their portfolios in stocks of non-U.S. companies. That meant Jan needed to develop our research on managers—mostly based in London—who invested internationally. We already knew how to do that based on our experience in the United States, and, at different times, we sent Dick Lothrop, Madelyn Smith, Helane Grill, Joan Sobba, and Don Hardy to guide Jan as he was getting started.

The United Kingdom had a highly developed pension industry, but it was, if anything, even more relationship-driven than the U.S. industry had been 10 years earlier. We would go in and ask managers our standard questions, such as, "What is your investment process?" They didn't understand the question; British managers weren't thinking in terms of process yet, so they couldn't answer it.

In 1981, Jan hired Mike Phillips, an Englishman who had been working as a portfolio manager at Barclays Bank in London. A dozen years later, Mike succeeded me as CEO. But in his first days at Frank Russell Company, Mike accompanied Jan on money manager interviews. He recalls,

> We asked one manager, "How do you pick stocks?" He looked at us quite intensely and said, "Very carefully, old boy." In another case, we asked a manager what technology he used. He gestured toward his head and said, "This is the best computer; I don't need anything else." Then he pointed at his trash can and added, "That's my filing system."

As in New York, we found it was not difficult to get interviews. Most of the managers understood that our U.S. clients had significant assets. By this time, pension funds that we were advising, such as United Airlines, Xerox, and IBM, had already committed to international strategies, so managers had a financial incentive to have meaningful conversations with us.

The second part of our strategy was to add new clients based in Europe. Our initial targets were the European subsidiaries of our U.S. consulting clients. For example, Rank Xerox and Caterpillar had operations in both the UK and Belgium. Next, Jan began pursuing UK pension funds. This was a somewhat longer slog, but, by the time he returned to the United States in 1984, Jan had secured a total of 15 retainer clients.

Our Battle to Exceed Client Expectations

By expanding into Europe, we were able to increase the size of our consulting practice by more than one-third. The 40-client limit applied only to the United States, and we had added a non-U.S. manager research capability, so our existing clients viewed our expansion overseas as a service enhancement.

However, like our real estate capability, the London office was another long-term investment. Frankly, during the first 25 years of the Russell organization, we didn't pay much attention to the bottom line: We couldn't have provided the quality of service that we needed to if we'd had a bottom-line focus.

Our Tokyo office is a case in point. It was our third office outside the U.S., so we had experience in starting an international operation when we opened it in 1986. Tokyo, however, was unique in that the existing laws prevented pension funds from investing outside Japan. Essentially, we committed ourselves to 10 years of red ink while we lobbied to change the law. Eventually, we came to represent six of the 10 largest companies in Japan, which never could have happened if we had constantly worried about the bottom line.

Ignoring the bottom line isn't as easy as you might think. As the head count grew at Frank Russell Company, we began to have more people who had a bottom-line focus. Now, I understand the need for profitability as well as anyone. But I found that an increasing number of associates were arguing that it was costing too much to exceed client expectations. After a lot of debate, I conceded the point and we adopted a new philosophy: We will *meet or exceed* client expectations. That lasted about 60 days and then I killed it. The reason is simple. Wherever the client sets the expectation level, if you deliver below it, the client will talk to all their friends and say you didn't do a very good job. If you meet expectations they will say nothing. But if you exceed their expectations, then they will start recommending you. Which one do you want?

Clearly, exceeding expectations was key to Russell's culture. But we still had to answer the question: How could we grow, given that we'd promised to limit our U.S. roster to 40 clients? Our London initiative permitted us to add new clients in Europe. But as I explained, the startup costs were high and it took quite a few years for that venture to become profitable. Quite honestly, our resources were so stretched that it was becoming difficult to retain some of our people.

A Funny Thing Happened on May 1, 1980

The answer came, as it usually does, out of the blue. Burlington Industries was one of our original clients. Right after we began consulting to JCPenney, Paul Kaltinick introduced me to the treasurer at Burlington Industries. In 1980, I still handled their account personally. I was meeting with their pension staff in New York City, and they mentioned that they had just merged with a smaller company that had a $35 million pension fund. Of course, that's a lot of money, but Burlington's fund had $2 billion in assets, which was more typical of the size needed for our consulting service to be cost effective. We had picked 18 different managers for Burlington's fund and we were monitoring all of them quite closely, as was our practice.

Because of some legal complication that I never fathomed, Burlington could not merge the fund of the new subsidiary into a single master trust along with its much larger, existing pension plan. They looked at me and said, "What are you going to do about this $35 million fund?"

I thought in silence for about one minute. Then I said, "We'll set up a trust company and use the same managers that you already have. We'll combine your equity managers in a fund called

Equity I; two or three bond managers in Fixed I; and we'll use another three or four managers in International I. If other companies have the same problem you do, we can commingle the assets and these funds will become a useful product."

That is the origin of our fund management business, which today is by far the single biggest part of Frank Russell Company in terms of its profit and its future prospects. As usual, it didn't start with vision. It started because one of our clients had a problem—and I had an intuitive reaction to the problem. And then I followed my usual practice of hiring smarter people to implement the idea with a solution.

It was an exciting time, because this idea of packaging our consulting strategies into funds clearly offered a way to increase our revenue growth. By definition, consulting is a service that has to be customized for each client. That business model doesn't scale. However, selling a fund to a theoretically unlimited number of smaller pension funds could get us out of that box, because our fees would increase along with assets under management. So we could bring in more revenue as we added new clients. And we'd also benefit as our clients' assets grew as a result of market advances and, presumably, the value we could add through our investment skill.

In addition, the fund model would allow us to bring the benefits of risk management to a much broader segment of pension funds. This is where ERISA really helped us because, of course, it applied equally to small pension funds with only a couple of million to invest, as well as a huge fund like IBM with several billion dollars' worth of assets. The principles of diversification still applied.

The Only Difference is the Zeros

By this time, we had developed our signature process that became known as *M-cubed*. *M* stands for *multi-* and *cubed* refers to the three levels of diversification that are optimal for managing market risk.

The first level is *multi-asset* class diversification. We accomplished this by adding "new" asset classes like international equities and real estate to a traditional portfolio of U.S. stocks, bonds, and cash.

The second level is *multi-style.* Thanks to our ability to classify managers as *growth* or *value* (or additional styles we identified later), we were able to mitigate the risk within the U.S. equity asset class. Fixed income, international, and real estate also have styles, enabling us to implement style diversification across the board.

The third level is *multi-manager* diversification. Like markets, organizations are constantly changing. Sometimes this change is not for the better, so we try to diversify managers to avoid becoming too dependent on the fortunes of a single firm.

As I noted, Burlington Industries' strategy required 18 distinct asset management firms to achieve proper diversification. From a smaller pension fund's perspective, that's a lot of relationships to manage and monitor. It's also expensive. And in many cases, high investment minimums would prevent these smaller funds from accessing quality managers.

Our commingled funds were a way for midsized plan sponsors to bypass these obstacles and obtain the kind of professional risk management stipulated by ERISA. When you think about it, it was a perfect fit. Our investment process was really "the right way to do it" for funds of all sizes. The phrase, *the only difference is the zeros,* encapsulates this insight: M-cubed works equally well for $100 billion, $100 million, $10 million, or $10,000. The same economies of scale that allowed us to address our revenue problem also allowed us to make M-cubed work for a much broader swath of investors. I liked the fact that entering the funds business wasn't just the profitable thing to do, but also the right thing to do.

Making It Fly

In Chapter 1, I described how I explained our new venture to each of our consulting clients individually. It was gratifying to see that we had earned their trust, because we needed their support before we could move forward.

However, we still had major legal obstacles to overcome. Nobody had ever done anything like this before. Sure, there were mutual funds. But that structure was designed for the average small individual investor. We needed something specific to the needs of institutions seeking to comply with ERISA.

That meant talking to lawyers—*lots* of them. I remember a meeting I held in New York when I was trying to figure out how to put this whole thing together. Frankly, the legal aspects of establishing and licensing a trust company are outside my area of expertise—I didn't know beans about it—so I borrowed a conference room at Citibank and brought in experts from Milbank, Tweed, Hadley & McCloy, a big legal firm in New York City, and Stradley Ronon Stevens & Young, which became our long-term mutual fund legal consultant, out of Philadelphia. I also flew in a lawyer from Tacoma, who specialized in bank funds.

As always, I wanted to move quickly. And there were about 14 people around the table—14 highly paid attorneys—so you could almost hear the meter chiming, minute by minute, in increments of $1,000.

The room had lots of free wall space, so we put a lot of blank charts around. I stood in front of these people: my legal team that I had never met before, except for the ones from Stradley Ronon. I pulled my car keys out of my pocket and held them where everyone could see them. I said, "These are the keys to the restroom and as soon as we have answers to my questions then I'll give them to you. What I need to know is how do we go forward? What are the action steps to get this idea formalized? What roles will the three of you assume? And how much is it going to cost me? Now let's get moving."

It took them about three hours to get answers. I gave them the restroom keys and we were able to open the doors of Frank Russell Trust Company on October 1, 1980.

We were lucky that the legal team included Phil Fina from Stradley Ronon. Phil is an example of a business attorney—all too rare these days—who focuses on finding ways to get things done, rather than avoiding all risk. I later hired him to work as our in-house counsel and he was famous for saying in meetings, "Tell me what you want to accomplish and I'll get back to you tomorrow and tell you how to do it." Phil gets the credit for convincing the banking commission in Washington State that it'd really be all right to charter us as a non-depository trust company.

About a year later, we realized we needed a separate legal structure so we could provide investment management services to individuals. Phil made it possible for us to open the doors of Frank Russell Investment Management Company in October 1981.

From the beginning, our investment management business had a strong value proposition. We were offering investors of all types and sizes access to the same managers and strategies that the very biggest, most sophisticated corporations were using. The M-cubed approach lowers risk, and it is the responsible way to manage money.

Despite our compelling story, there was a lot of inertia to overcome. Even though we had the experience and tools to do a much better job of managing risk than the internal staff of almost any pension fund, it must have felt to them that they were losing contact with their managers. In some cases, I honestly felt that the pension committees and their staff enjoyed the excitement of investing and didn't want to give it up.

We also had to deal with the challenge of index funds, which were coming into vogue at that time. Instead of investing a great deal of money into researching stocks or managers who are trying to beat the market, index funds simply buy all of the stocks in an index like the S&P 500 and charge only a small fraction of the fees that are typical of an active manager. As a result, we now had a target—and a difficult one at that. We had to beat the market return, net of fees, to prove that we were adding value.

FRTC's All-Stars

To address these two challenges of inertia on the one hand and a low-cost competitor on the other, I knew we needed to add talented people with specialized skills. Our first big breakthrough came when Paul Kaltinick agreed to join us as CEO of Frank Russell Trust Company (FRTC).

Paul found the Russell funds concept compelling when he visited us during the summer of 1980. I took him on a boat ride on the waters of Puget Sound on a spectacular evening when Mt. Rainier seemed to hover within arm's reach against a rich blue curtain. I explained the value proposition and asked him his opinion of the two finalists I was considering for CEO. When he finished looking at the resumes, Paul half-jokingly said, "Well, what about me?" I half-jokingly replied, "Are you interested?"

As a client, Paul had always been a powerful advocate for Frank Russell Company. I'd say he was a catalyst for many of our most significant accomplishments. So you can imagine how good I felt when he took the reins of Frank Russell Trust Company in the fall of 1980.

Our next task was building a sales force. Ten years earlier, I had personally built our roster of 40 clients. After that, we generally had a waiting list of companies who were eager to take the next available slot.

However, the market for our investment funds was entirely different. In the first place, we now had thousands of prospects that we had to contact and cultivate. That's why we assigned Dick Lothrop to build and manage a new professional sales force for our funds business. Along with Jim Martin, Virginia Sirusis, and Jim Vogelzang, Dick hired Brandy Nielsen, who came from Prudential, where he had been instrumental in selling the PRISA real estate fund. Our new professional sales force understood that selling to institutional investors required sustained education and relationship building over a period of years—a process that Brandy used to call "hovering."

On the investment side, we had written the book about selecting and combining managers. But managing managers on a day-to-day basis required an additional set of skills. Indexing was a shot across our bow, and we knew we needed to bring our M-cubed model to a new level of sophistication and precision.

In 1981, Madelyn Smith hired a young man named Dennis Trittin, right out of the University of Washington's graduate program. In his work on U.S. equity managers, Dennis felt that it wasn't enough to simply "avoid the left tail," in other words, to stay away from managers whose performance was below average in a statistical distribution. Dennis wanted to develop the ability to *forecast* which managers would be able to beat their passive benchmarks. He worked with his team to build various models to analyze process characteristics and identify the ones with the most predictive power.

The next step was portfolio construction, which required us to optimize the manager mix with more precision than we'd been able to achieve in the past. Randy Lert spearheaded this effort after he joined us in 1985. Randy's previous experience was at Wells Fargo, so he had a solid understanding of the challenge that indexing represented for us. In Randy's words:

> We needed to focus more on the overall structure of the portfolio and its characteristics versus its benchmark index. We needed to find out if we had, inadvertently, put in place some long-term bets against the index. Today, we start by identifying the characteristics we want the fund to have. What are its factor exposures? What is our tolerance for deviation from the benchmark? Once we know what we want the portfolio to look like, then we start to look at which highly ranked managers might be a good fit. Finally, we use optimization tools to determine the manager structure most likely to achieve the intended result.

With Randy as our chief investment officer and Dennis as portfolio manager, our flagship Equity I Fund achieved a remarkable record of beating its benchmark, the Russell 1000 Index, by a considerable margin for every calendar year consecutively from 1989 to 1996. Most of the other funds were also doing well, and this gave Brandy Nielsen the confidence to start approaching larger pension funds than he had before—those with assets in the range of $500 million to $1 billion.

His proposal was a bold one: He suggested that companies outsource their entire pension fund operation to Russell's management. He'd been "hovering" around Kaiser Aluminum for more than 10 years, building a relationship with Norm van Patten, who was Kaiser's director of pension fund management. Finally, in 1994, van Patten said yes, giving Frank Russell Trust Company a key outsourcing mandate.

In my mind, this is the moment when our funds business began to live up to its potential. We had shown the market we could provide enough value both to beat the passive benchmark and to overcome the plan sponsor's natural reluctance to give up day-to-day control over significant company assets.

From Wall Street to Main Street

One year to the day after forming Frank Russell Trust Company, we created the second part of our investment business, Frank Russell Investment Management Company (FRIMCo). FRIMCo's mission was to bring the M-cubed model to the world at large: smaller pension plans, non-ERISA accounts such as endowments and foundations, and individual investors.

In some respects, this was an easier task than launching the Trust Company. We had already been through the process once, and the legal challenges were not as difficult. We were able to set up our FRIMCo offerings as mutual funds, which didn't require us to establish any groundbreaking precedents.

The challenge of national distribution was a different matter. Doing it ourselves was out of the question. It would have cost too much and taken too long to gain traction. A far wiser strategy was to align ourselves with partners who already had relationships with our target market.

We started with regional banks. Some of our first clients included Union Trust in Connecticut and People's Bank in Seattle. People's Bank is a great example. In the early 1980s, they were the fourth largest bank in Washington State. They did have some in-house portfolio management capabilities, but not much market penetration. I went to visit them and spoke with Steve Davis, their employee benefits director. As Steve recalls:

> We were really excited. We saw this as an instant way to be credible in the employee benefit market. Becoming a Russell distributor gave us a way to attract clients and provide them with a first-class investment product. It was an ideal solution for a small bank like we were. Now we could provide small pools of capital—like a doctor or dentist's retirement account—with the same strategies that IBM was using.

People's Bank didn't stay small for very long. They experienced a lot of success selling Russell funds in their market. And then U.S. Bank acquired them in 1987, which was a windfall for FRIMCo. Not long after the acquisition, Steve marched up to the boardroom and made the pitch that U.S. Bank ought to invest the assets in its own DB plan into Russell Funds. The board made the right decision and FRIMCo gained approximately $30 million in assets under management. Eventually, U.S. Bank became our biggest bank relationship, with more than $1.6 billion invested with us.

Unfortunately, when it comes to bank mergers, what goes around comes around. In 1997, U.S. Bank was acquired by First Bank, based in Minneapolis, and the new corporate parent clearly favored its own internally managed products. This is the nature of the banking industry.

Our next initiative within FRIMCo was to seek out independent investment advisors who could sell the M-cubed investment process to a clientele composed primarily of individual investors. The Russell Advisors program is near and dear to my heart, because independent advisors tend to be entrepreneurs and peddlers—like me.

Russ Hill is one of our most productive and creative Russell Advisors. He's president and CEO of Halbert Hargrove in Long Beach, California. Russ recalls reading about our Atlanta affiliate, Reiser-Builder, Inc., in the old *Pensions & Investment Age*. Russ immediately saw the advantages of an association with our firm, and he called right away. Our head of sales and marketing, Tony Whatley, took the call and suggested Russ look him up next time he was in the area. Russ replied, "That's strange, because I am going to be in Tacoma tomorrow. Do you have any time?"

As you'll recall, I used the same gambit when I set up my first appointment with JCPenney in 1969.

Russ made a great first impression, and there was no doubting his experience or talent. But we still made him go through a rigorous process that we referred to internally as putting the candidate *in the box*. This consisted of days of interviews and casual interactions with as many Russell associates as possible—similar to our internal hiring discipline. In addition, advisors had to go through a series of focus groups, each of which represented a type of prospect: wealthy families, doctors, lawyers, CPAs, and so forth. Usually there were four groups with 10 people in each. As Russ recalls, "Those focus groups were one of the least pleasant experiences of my life, wondering if I could get 40 people in different categories to think I was a good guy." In fact, the focus groups were little different than conducting a seminar for potential investors, and of course Russ passed with flying colors. More importantly, the whole process was designed to select individuals and firms that were a good cultural fit with the Russell organization.

Bill Rice of Anchor Capital in Boston already had a thriving business when we first contacted him in 1987. In our initial discussions, he was leery about trying to convert existing clients to a different service model. So I went to Boston to talk to him, and a 10-minute meeting turned into a two-hour conversation. In the course of that wide-ranging dialogue we discovered we had three or four things in common: First, we were both peddlers. Second, we had actually met before. In 1969, Bill had started a money management firm called Endowment Management and Research (EM&R) and I had researched them in the early days of the consulting business—and even recommended him to clients! Third, we both understood the value of bringing manager oversight, disciplined asset allocation, and style diversification to investors of all types and sizes. Fourth, and most important, we both had a similar view about culture.

Anchor had a very tightly knit team and little or no employee turnover over long periods of time. Bill obviously liked the fact that our culture had similar qualities:

> Russell's culture was paternalistic, caring about people. You could tell Russell people took pride in their work and in the fact that the Frank Russell Company name was associated with the highest standards of professionalism, integrity, and industry smarts. It made us feel good about being associated with them. We were concerned about linking the Anchor name with Russell's, just as Russell was concerned about linking with us. Over time, we came to see that our cultures were immensely compatible and very parallel.

The advisor model has been very successful in expanding Russell's investment process to a much broader clientele.

Concentric Circles

It's interesting to see how far a single, simple idea can take you, once it starts gathering momentum. Our original insight was that utilizing one or two managers selected because of relationships was no way to build an investment program. So we developed a manager research capability and began recommending multi-manager strategies.

Then we began to recommend adding new asset classes, including international equities and real estate. We extended our research process to these new types of managers and opened an office in London to replicate in Europe what we already were doing in the U.S.

Our work in the U.S. showed us that there were multiple styles of equity managers, so we again extended our process to growth and value, and large and small cap managers.

Next, we noticed that the tools we'd developed to analyze managers for our consulting clients, including performance universes and equity profiles, would help money managers to understand the links between their process and portfolio and their ultimate results. In 1972, we started a data business headed by Dick Lothrop to sell those tools more broadly.

I just related the story of how we created our funds business by cloning a client's strategy for a smaller subsidiary. This allowed us to address the middle market of pension plans.

Then we realized that we could do the same for individual investors and institutions not governed by ERISA, such as endowments and foundations. We had to create a separate subsidiary with a mutual fund structure, but still follow the same M-cubed investment process. And we partnered with a variety of distributors including banks, independent advisors, and, eventually, brokerage firms such as A.G. Edwards and Raymond James.

Now we were leveraging our core intellectual capital, which is our manager research, into all segments of the U.S. market. Finally, our funds were giving us a way to capitalize on our seemingly fantastic forays into real estate and non-U.S. equities.

But what about the international offices? After starting with offshore offices in London, Toronto, Tokyo, and Sydney, we eventually expanded to Amsterdam, Auckland, Johannesburg, Melbourne, Paris, Singapore, and Zurich. As in the U.S., we began with manager research and consulting to local pension funds and, from that foundation, launched fund complexes following our M-cubed model— of course.

Interestingly, as our funds business grew, we began to notice an unanticipated side benefit: Randy, Dennis, and other members of the portfolio management team were developing ancillary strategies to reduce expenses from trading commissions, and to increase returns through innovative programs such as *equitizing* residual cash that can put a drag on a portfolio because it's not producing the market return. Now we were able to repay our consulting clients' trust, by introducing them to the money-saving techniques that our funds group had developed, creating a virtuous circle. As Dennis puts it, "Russell's investment management operation makes us a much better consultant, and our consulting practice makes us a much better investment manager."

My point is that business creativity doesn't necessarily require a breakthrough innovation each time. It can be a simple variation on a theme or having the courage to enter a new market. You may simply be leveraging an existing idea, but it still takes creativity to make everything work: Creativity is required to solve problems in all functional areas, including legal, operations, and sales—it's not limited to product development.

However you define it, creativity is critically important to your success. If you always follow what everybody else does, it is obvious that you cannot lead. And if you do not lead, you will never experience the excitement of evolution and growth in your business.

Key Points from Chapter 4

1. You don't have to pay a lot of money for creativity. Creativity will emerge naturally if you support it as part of your business culture.
2. Creative ideas may be ahead of the market. It requires patience and a willingness to ignore the bottom line when you're waiting for the market to catch up.
3. Not every idea is a breakthrough innovation. Often it's enough to introduce an established product to a new market.
4. Don't forget about sales. A truly new idea may be hard to understand or may require changing old habits. You need to educate the market.
5. Remember, your competitors are creative, too. Be prepared to respond to strategic inflection points so you can remain relevant.

CHAPTER

Work Hard

"PUT ASSOCIATES FIRST—AND THEY'LL TAKE CARE OF THE CLIENTS."

know what you're thinking. Why do you need me, or anyone else, to tell you to work hard? Everyone in business expects to work hard. However, at Russell, we made a conscious decision to avoid the grueling workaholic culture of many New York financial institutions. Devoting 16-hour days and frequent weekends to work doesn't leave very much time for family, relaxation, or developing other sides of yourself. I wanted our associates to work really hard for eight hours at the office and then go home and focus on their families. My thought was that we all have three eight-hour sessions during the day: one for sleep, one for work, and one for home. If you shortchange any of these, there are bound to be consequences.

To put it another way, we were asking people to *focus* for eight hours each day during a five-day week. A focused 40 hours of work is better than 60 hours without focus. We wanted that good, solid 40; beyond that, we didn't want to see you in the building— except in special cases, like a major deadline.

We cared about our people and their well-being. If someone was sick or had a family emergency or critical commitment, we did not want that person to come to work. Our philosophy was *family comes first*. We expected our associates to take care of themselves and their issues, and then come back when they could work without distractions.

That's the theory. Now let's look at how our culture of working hard actually worked.

Setting the Tone

I wouldn't be candid if I didn't tell you that many Russell associates believe that I always kept a ferocious pace—and expected them to do the same.

If you ask Madelyn Smith or Helane Grill what it was like going on a road trip with me, they'll probably say they get a headache just thinking about it.

Jeannette Kirschman describes a trip that I booked for her in the winter of 1978. I scheduled appointments in Pittsburgh, Detroit, Chicago, St. Louis, and Dallas. Though I don't think it's fair to hold me responsible for the nine-degree weather in Detroit or the snowstorm in Dallas, Jeannette will still say, "That was the first and last time George was responsible for planning my itinerary."

Ask Blake Eagle and he'll tell you how I hired a cab to drive 200 miles to Peoria because the St. Louis airport was fogged in. Or the time I ordered a forced march, two and a half miles on foot to Allis-Chalmers' headquarters in Milwaukee, because taxis couldn't make it through 20 inches of snow.

Then there's the story Don Ezra tells about showing me around Toronto for the first time after we opened our office there:

> George visited us on our first anniversary. He planned to stay
> for three days. Jan Twardowski warned me, "Keep him busy.
> Do not give him a spare moment. He goes absolutely crazy if
> he has nothing to do."

I think what Jan meant to say was that I don't like to waste time. In any case, Don continues:

> So we put together a nonstop agenda, meeting and talking to all kinds of people: clients, prospects, government agencies. We had to take taxis everywhere because we were always short of time.

When it was time to leave, we all shook hands and I told them they were doing a great job and that I felt the same kind of excitement we had in Tacoma at the start. Don recalls that he was beaming—as he had every right to be. Then he adds,

> As the elevator doors were sliding shut, George said, "Just one thing—next time, try to keep things moving." My jaw dropped: *Keep things moving? What do you think we've been doing?*

These anecdotes do a good job of capturing my reputation around the company. I was definitely trying to set a strong, positive example. That's a leader's responsibility. You can't ask people to do something you're not willing to do yourself. In my case, it wasn't a problem. I like to work hard. And I didn't mind putting in long hours—when I was *traveling*.

When I first started selling the consulting service, there was one trip where we met with 33 different prospects in six cities in the course of a single week. I call that efficient planning. The idea is simply to get as much done as possible, so you can get home as soon as possible. When you're on the road, you can't go home at five o'clock, so it's a great time to work 16-hour days if you need to. You're not missing out on time with family members.

I compare the two work modes—home and travel—to the kind of energy you have to put out in my favorite sports—wrestling and mountain climbing. In wrestling, you focus your efforts in a confined space for a concentrated amount of time. Then you're done. You take your shower and go home. Ideally, you've won your match. Hopefully the team won. Mountain climbing requires a more sustained effort. You are far from home and the territory is wide open. You know the objective and the route you expect to take. But you never know what you'll encounter along the way. If you don't make enough progress the first day, you may have to make up for it the next day. Maybe you'll need to start at midnight to reach the summit by 10 A.M. the next morning—and then get back down safely. Obviously, *work hard* is a flexible standard. It's not like integrity, which has to be non-negotiable, because a single slip can bring down the entire enterprise. Working extra hours may be necessary depending on the circumstances, which include job requirements, stages of the company's development, and individual work styles.

For a leader, setting a personal example of the organization's work ethic is the critical first step. I knew the message was getting through about staying busy and focused at work. But it's harder to model the part about spending quality time with your family. After all, the point is to leave work behind as completely as possible.

Our family used to enjoy traveling by boat in the inside passage between Vancouver and mainland British Columbia. It's only a couple of hundred miles from Tacoma, but the rugged coastline makes it impassible by car, so you arrive in pristine country quite quickly. In the summertime, when the weather in the Pacific Northwest is close to perfect, cruising those waters with my wife, Jane, and our four children was relaxing and restorative. I probably should have found a way to share with associates a bit more of this type of experience, to communicate the importance of life apart from work.

There was one time, however, when I did need to make a work-related phone call while we were cruising across the Strait of Georgia. Those were the days before cell phones—and it's doubtful you could find service in such a remote spot even today. We docked at a small town on Vancouver Island and I found my way to the only pay phone. The call took nearly an hour and, by the time I was through, there was a line of people annoyed at me for tying up the phone. I decided not to tell them it takes more than a minute or two to negotiate the price of a seat on the New York Stock Exchange.

The 120 Percent People

Hiring direct reports who share your attitude about work is the next key step in propagating the culture. Madelyn Smith, Joan Sobba, and Peter Dietz all had different work styles, and each one was successful in a different way.

Madelyn quickly realized that my whirlwind trips and five meetings per day did not suit her. The more we learned about managers, the more detailed our research visits had to be. As a result, they took more time. Madelyn felt that the optimal number for her was three a day. When she wasn't traveling, Madelyn was very disciplined and focused on the job. Most days she was able to leave work by five, which, as she was a single mother, was a necessity.

Madelyn did an excellent job hiring and managing young research analysts as our staff in this area grew to around 50 people. Over the years she noted with surprise, and a bit of frustration, that her people would complain about the three-a-day regime she'd established. So they cut it back to two. Again, I attribute this decrease in the number of meetings to the growing complexity of the research process. But I also interpret it as a sign that the culture was working as intended.

Peter Dietz had a very different work style. He welcomed and initiated a lot of extraneous conversation while at work. He was extremely sociable and, as an academic, brought a different frame of reference to work than many of us with a purely business background. As a result of his unfocused style, he often had to stay late to get things done. Of course, this didn't mean he was working harder. It was just something everyone understood and accepted. As director of R&D, Peter was responsible for hiring many of the brilliant people who helped develop our intellectual capital. And his personal work style did not necessarily carry over to the people he hired. Again, I interpret this as a sign that our culture was working.

Joan Sobba probably had the most difficult job in the company because she had to work so closely with me. She had her own set of responsibilities in addition to managing my active schedule and many commitments. When I talked to her about this chapter, her voice got low and serious. She said that she doubted she *ever* worked as few as 40 hours in a week during her 30 years at the company.

As the company grew, we tried to give Joan the resources she needed to get everything done in the time available. In 1974, we hired Joan Lichtenberg, who worked for Dick Lothrop for one year and earned the nickname "Lightning." By October 1975, I needed Joan Sobba's help in a client relationship role, so I stole Lightning away from Dick as my personal secretary. From this point on, I had both Joans working extremely hard. Lightning's job had an internal focus. In addition to managing my contacts and schedule, she also kept track of every assignment, reminding each team member of their due dates and responsibilities. That's not easy. Lightning had a wonderful ability to work with some huge egos, to keep calm and take nothing personally. Lightning was indispensable. I was lucky to have her working at my side through most of my career.

Theoretically, Lightning's presence freed up some extra time for Joan Sobba; but as I explained in the "Three Musketeers" section in Chapter 3, Joan's growing responsibilities always kept her busy. Somehow, she still managed to live a balanced life, as her accomplishments as a horsewoman and world traveler attest. Joan and I are very similar in terms of energy and attitude toward work. She reminded me of a story from our early days together that I had completely forgotten: One afternoon, Joan told me she needed to leave early to go to an appointment. I said that was fine—particularly as it happened so rarely. By coincidence, I had to leave early that day, as well. In fact, Joan and I ended up leaving the office at about the same time.

Imagine our surprise when we both found ourselves at the same "appointment." We were both in a class for *remedial drivers' education*—the result of too many tickets for being in too great a hurry driving to and from work. I interpreted that as a sign of the culture not quite living up to its potential!

Joan used to look for "120 percent people" when she was filling positions at the company. That's another way of talking about focus. If you shoot for 100 percent, you inevitably will be distracted a certain amount of the time and end up giving only 80 percent. That's why you had to shoot for 120 percent, in order to arrive at the goal of 100 percent.

When business leaders set the right example, word gets around. As Brian Barker, one of our institutional salespeople, recalls:

> Nobody waved a finger at you and said, "Go on a sales trip to Chicago." You simply understood the work ethic; you stayed in your office and did whatever it took to get your meetings scheduled—because that was your job. It wasn't prescribed; it was leadership.

For the most part, the culture was self-enforcing. We didn't have to fire too many people. If they didn't like our work ethic or couldn't keep pace, they generally seemed to leave on their own. As a result, Frank Russell Company was populated with 120 percent people, and that's a big part of the reason why we were successful.

Work is Only a Means to an End

After setting a personal example of the work ethic and hiring key people who buy into that philosophy, the next step is to make sure your associates understand what all the hard work is for. I mentioned earlier that our objective was to exceed client expectations. That's a general statement—deliberately so—which makes it possible for people in different parts of the company to apply it to their specific tasks.

Getting a client report ready for delivery was always a major event. As much as we tried to stay on schedule, between writing, editing, and creating diagrams as new data were coming in, we always seemed to find ourselves collating and binding the reports fairly late the night before they were due. Everybody used to lend a hand. One of them was John James, who, over the years, held senior positions in administration, HR, and sales. In the early days, John worked for Bondstock and had no responsibilities in the area of our consulting practice. Yet when a report was due, John used to come in and help Joan and the rest of us. He particularly remembers using an X-acto knife to scrape off stray marks left by the Xerox machine. Quality control was one way in which we aimed to exceed client expectations, and everyone pulled together toward that goal.

Another example is the work Janine Baldridge and her associates used to do in our performance reporting area. We hired Janine in 1979 as a management trainee and she later worked her way up to become one of our senior consultants. Janine recalls how, in those days, performance measurement was a painstaking process. We had a product called Portfolio Activity Report (PAR). We had to get the data on our clients' transactions from their custodian and clean it up. Only then could we apply Peter Dietz's formula for calculating investment returns. The issue was that there were numerous errors in these basic transaction records. As a result, our performance measurement service incorporated a complete audit of every single transaction in our clients' multibillion-dollar pension fund accounts! Hard work? You bet. But it was worth it. Our audits alone resulted in millions of dollars in savings—amounts that exceeded our consulting fees by a wide margin. As an added bonus, Janine observes:

> Russell's verification process was instrumental in actually getting banks to set up better auditing and accounting procedures. It was embarrassing for them to get quarterly letters from us. . . . Or in particularly egregious cases, they might even get a call saying, "Where is that two-million-dollar contribution our client made?"

Portfolio verification was hard work. Nobody else was doing it, and it needed to get done. I can assure you our clients appreciated it; they certainly never expected to realize an immediate ROI from hiring a consultant.

If I can offer one more example of a hard worker, it's Bobbie Gayton, who was our receptionist for many years. Sitting at the front desk, Bobbie was usually the first person to greet clients visiting us in Tacoma. Like many professional receptionists, Bobbie had a real talent for remembering names and faces. But she also interpreted her job responsibilities in a uniquely personal way. When visitors had to wait in the lobby, Bobbie would engage them in conversation and, if they seemed receptive, she'd provide a quick guided tour. She'd point out our building's features such as its orientation toward Mt. Rainier, and share details about the medallions representing our international offices or my collection of mountaineering books. Not only was this a kindness to people who might need or enjoy a warm welcome after traveling, it was a discreet way of introducing our values, which provide the foundation for good business relationships.

Though their jobs were very different, John James, Janine Baldridge, and Bobbie Gayton all worked hard to deliver service that would make a positive lasting impression on our clients. In this way, they provide a pretty fair representation of how we expected our associates to act—and most of them followed suit.

Incentives that Worked

There's no doubt that helping clients improve financial security is a worthwhile enterprise. It's the kind of work that people can take pride in. And a lot of the time it's intellectually satisfying as well. But we would have been naïve to suppose that we could have attracted and retained the kind of people we needed if our compensation and benefits were not generous enough. If you want people to work hard over a long period of time, you definitely need to put the right incentives in place.

I look at it this way: You have to take good care of your employees because otherwise they will spend a certain percentage of their time worrying about their future—retirement benefits, health care, and so forth. These preoccupations would detract from what otherwise would be 100 percent attention to the client. However, if we answer all of those personal questions in advance by making them feel financially secure, then they're free to focus on the client situation. That's why I repeated the phrase so frequently, "We put our associates first."

I'm extremely proud of the fact that Russell won several high-profile awards for being an employee-friendly workplace. Nationally, we ranked in the top 15 of *Fortune* magazine's 100 Best Companies to Work For competition, each year from 1999 to 2002. And we've won *Washington CEO*'s designation "Best Large Company to Work for in Washington State" on three separate occasions. Along with our exceptional employee-retention numbers, this recognition helps validate our success in putting the right incentives in place.

Before I describe our core employee benefits, I want to describe some of the small gestures we incorporated into our culture: On birthdays, all Russell associates receive a flower delivered right to their desk. After five years of service, they receive a life-sized brass apple; after that they receive monetary gifts, starting at $500 at 10 years and increasing to $2,000—and a company-sponsored celebration—at 20 years. The milestones keep increasing at five-year intervals. After 35 years, the bonus is $3,500 and a fairly lavish party! These gifts play a big role in communicating that we care about our people—as individuals.

Obviously, we needed to have a world-class retirement plan as the centerpiece of our benefits package. We provided associates with a broad selection of well-diversified investment vehicles, in the form of Frank Russell Trust Company funds, and we also waived the management fee. In addition, we supplemented associates' salary deferrals with a discretionary company contribution of as much as 15 percent of pay. Fifteen percent is the maximum allowed by law, and it was discretionary in the sense that we probably would not have made the contribution in the event of a bad year. However, I regarded the contribution as a more-or-less fixed cost that was part of treating associates the right way. And, in fact, Russell did commit the maximum every year during my tenure.

I used to announce the award of the discretionary contribution in December at our annual meeting. As business was typically slow during the holidays, I'd sometimes announce an extra day off with pay. You wouldn't believe the cheers and applause—much louder and more enthusiastic than the way they'd greeted the announcement of the discretionary contribution.

One time, I decided to say something about it. I told the associates that, as professionals in the retirement industry, they must understand the value of these annual 15 percent contributions, compounding without taxes or fees for decades. Yet they gave that a *ho-hum* response—and then went crazy for a little thing like an extra day off.

Maybe we were working them too hard.

I gave that some thought and discussed the matter with Jane. A year or two later, we added another benefit that really did get everyone's attention. It's a story that requires more than a paragraph or two: In fact, I'm making it the centerpiece of the final chapter, "Have Fun."

In the meanwhile, we tried to help associates take care of themselves with an excellent health benefits package that was premium-free after five years of service. Time off for vacation started at three weeks per year—not quite on a par with the Europeans, but quite generous by U.S. standards. In addition to the official HR policy, people understood that if they needed extra time off, they could get it.

We also recognized that many of the smart people we had in the organization would do best if they could pick their own challenges. Both Duncan Smith and Don Ezra, whom you met in Chapter 3, filled many roles during their lengthy tenures at Frank Russell Company. Duncan and Don had assignments involving management at different points, and performed at a high level. In fact, most companies would have required them to accept steadily increasing management responsibilities as their careers progressed. We would have done the same if headcount was what they had wanted. But neither of them did. Duncan and Don are doers and problem solvers; they came to me and told me that they'd prefer not to spend the best years of their professional lives managing people. So we created roles for them where they could add the most value to the company. It was an easy decision. It didn't cost us a dime—just the opposite, as both men became more productive. Giving people a sense of autonomy and authentic purpose is one of the most powerful incentives available to you as a business leader.

Of course, we weren't able to accommodate all of our associates' preferences as thoroughly as we did with Don and Duncan. But we did our best to provide career paths and opportunities to change assignments for anyone who could handle the responsibility.

My wife, Jane, who passed away in 2002 after a devastating bout with cancer, had much to do with designing Russell's approach to caring for its associates. She officially headed our "People Division" beginning in 1988, and always had a strong influence on the company and its people. Jane would walk the halls and talk to people directly. She'd ask them how they were doing and had an uncanny way of communicating that she really did care. For much of its history, Frank Russell Company truly had a family feel to it—as a place that took care of its own.

Growth and Change

After we entered the investment management business, it became more difficult to maintain the company's "family feel." Many people would argue that this was a good outcome, because families are about emotions and businesses are rational money-making machines. Personally, I wanted to have it both ways: Scale the business and scale the culture along with it.

I had no second thoughts about growing the company. Increasing our revenues and our impact on the market were all to the good. Growing headcount was fine as well, provided costs did not grow faster than revenues. I knew we would need people to make our strategy successful. During the decade of the 1980s, we increased the number of associates from 125 as a pension fund consultant to around 1,000 as we added our asset management capabilities. This was certainly a major change. When we were simply consultants, I never needed an organizational chart to run the company. As an asset manager, we had to have one.

The nature of our work changed as well. We were no longer entrepreneurs, pure and simple, because there was so much to do administratively. I found myself working, first, with Paul Kaltinick at the trust company and Don Powell heading the investment company, and then with Lynn Anderson, who came on in 1987 as CEO of both parts of our investment business. There were so many new issues to deal with. We had to create entire departments from scratch—operations, sales, client service, compliance, IT—and realign some of the responsibilities within manager research to ensure that both consulting and investment clients would be properly served. We also had more complex financial issues to manage, which we addressed by hiring Jim McDonald in 1985 to fill the CFO role.

Our consulting heritage stood us in good stead in the areas directly related to investing. We knew how to research managers and combine them in portfolios. We knew how to serve clients. But in other areas we were clearly playing catch-up. Randy Lert, who became chief investment officer of our funds, remembers thinking that we were underestimating the difficulty of mutual fund operations. He describes that particular challenge as: "Work, work, just daily *work*. Cash in, cash out. Accounting irregularities. Compliance issues. Working with managers on cash flow management. Work." That's why we brought in asset management specialists, including George Weber. We knew it was important to get it right.

In spite of my background as a peddler, our consulting culture definitely did not have a sales focus. So we had to create an institutional sales force, and spend the long hours needed over periods measured not in weeks or months, but years, to build our relationships.

Of course, our consulting practice continued to break new ground. In 1982, we prepared a mammoth report for General Motors at the request of Gordon Binns, who was one of the most influential institutional investors of our era. Then in 1984 came the consent decree that broke up AT&T into seven Baby Bells. That meant splitting one gigantic pension fund into seven merely enormous ones, which in turn meant long hours for the consultants who had been working with AT&T.

Also during this period, technology was starting to turn everything upside down, not just for us, but the entire industry. This was a trend we could not afford to ignore. In just a few years, we transitioned our data processing from ADP in New York to renting part of the facility at Puget Sound National Bank. From there we moved to Boeing. But that lasted only a year because IBM came out with a hot new "mini" mainframe called the 4331. We had to get that. Then something better came along, the NAS mainframe, so of course we upgraded. Don't even ask me about our Wang word-processing system, which we installed just as desktop computers were poised to render everything else obsolete. As the end of the millennium approached, we had nearly 200 people in our IT department. Their efforts resulted in the creation of important analytical tools such as our Sequential Equity Profile and AME (Analysis of Management Effect)—not to mention the Russell Indexes. And, fortunately, things eased off a bit after Y2K came and went.

Opening new global offices required plenty of legwork. While it was "easy" to leverage our intellectual capital, it takes a major effort to develop infrastructure and relationships on different continents. Today, Russell has nine principal offices located in New York, London, Tokyo, Paris, Singapore, Sydney, Auckland, Toronto, and Tacoma.

With our new CFO in place, we needed to develop new processes for planning, budgeting, and controlling the organization.

I guess we were lucky to get along so well, for so long, without these basic tools. Instituting a disciplined budget process was a lot of work, particularly as we developed a consensus-driven decision-making style. Jim McDonald also introduced management reporting by product, which required a somewhat controversial system of cost allocations. Not much fun—but it had to be done.

Global expansion in the funds business gave our legal team plenty to do. We started in Canada in 1993 and, in short order, started fund complexes domiciled in Ireland, the Cayman Islands, Australia, and Japan, with feeder funds in Israel, Italy, and Singapore. Also, the process of selling the company to Northwestern Mutual began in 1997 and continued until the deal closed at the beginning of 1999. That meant a heavy work-load for our general counsel, Karl Ege, along with Mike Phillips and Jim McDonald—all so I could stop working so hard.

While these changes were admittedly of a dramatic nature, I didn't see them as a reason to change the culture of the company. We still wanted to work hard in order to exceed client expectations. And that meant continuing to put associates first, because we knew it was the best way to motivate people to take proper care of our clients.

Lynn Anderson once observed that the reason *prospects* would choose to become Russell *clients* was because of our *people*. Says Lynn:

> We always felt that the best way to close a sale was to bring the prospect to Tacoma, to let them meet the people who do the work here. And, once they became clients and began to actually work with us, our people were able to build up a great reservoir of positive feelings that are the basis for solid, long-term relationships.

To me, Lynn's words show that our philosophy about work and incentives was right on target. I can't think of a better example of a corporate culture working exactly as it was designed to do.

Key Points from Chapter 5

1. Working hard is more about focus than the actual hours spent on the job.
2. Family time, and downtime in general, are essential. It's not healthy for employees to "live" at the office. However, there are exceptions when everyone needs to work overtime to help meet a deadline.
3. Lead by example. Don't ask people to do anything you're not willing to do yourself.
4. Hire good role models who can help you set the right tone, and in turn hire people who accept the company's work ethic.
5. Treat people well in general, and put the right financial incentives in place. People who are insecure about the future get distracted on the job.
6. People work harder and more effectively when they understand what they're working for and enjoy what they're doing.

CHAPTER 6

Share Credit

"AND CELEBRATE MISTAKES."

t's amazing what you can accomplish when you don't care who gets the credit. That's a phrase I have been using, rather happily, for quite a few years. It's a good thought; I knew that Ronald Reagan had once said something similar, but was quite surprised when I found out recently that the phrase has been around forever, more or less.

The earliest recorded usage is from British journalist Charles Montague in 1922. He wrote, "There is no limit to what a man can do so long as he does not care a straw who gets the credit for it." But teamwork is as old as human culture itself. Think of the organizational skills it took to bring together a band of hunters whose goal was to drive a bison herd over a cliff. No doubt our cave-dwelling ancestors had aphorisms on the subject as well. I think it's safe to say that sharing credit is a universal truth. However, it's a bit difficult to implement, which is why it has to be rediscovered from generation to generation—or even more frequently, in some cases.

Getting Rid of Titles

You can easily observe the power of sharing credit in the workplace. It's a simple matter of comparing the productivity of an egocentric person with that of someone who empowers his or her associates and places all bets on teamwork for a better solution. None of us has all the answers. And none of us has the capacity to do all the work that needs to be done. That's why we have organizations that are divided into different functional areas. Everyone has a job to do and, in my experience, when leaders share the credit, both the organization's productivity *and the client's satisfaction* doubles—at the very least.

That was my thought when in 1991 I noticed an unfortunate tendency at Russell. I felt we were following in the footsteps of the banks. We had more vice presidents than you could count. The titles seemed to start with assistant-assistant-assistant vice president; from there you could work your way up to executive vice president. I felt our people were paying too much attention to what their title was and not enough to getting work done for our clients. So I abolished all of those titles. I told people to invent their own titles. Most people chose functional titles, from what I hear: I never looked at most of them. There was a terrific amount of complaining for about a month-and-a-half or two months. Most of this came from the salespeople, who were afraid this might give an advantage to competitors who had impressive-sounding titles. I ignored that noise, and we still managed to win new business.

Stars of the Investment Industry

The peddlers did have a point, in the sense that there is a star system in the investment industry. For a while, everybody talked about Elaine Garzarelli because she successfully predicted the market break in 1987. Then there was Peter Lynch, whose performance at Magellan Fund propelled Fidelity's success for a decade or more. Abby Joseph Cohen was a star for Goldman Sachs throughout the amazing tech rally of the late 1990s. Even an industry curmudgeon like Jack Bogle became a household name, as Vanguard's S&P overtook Magellan to become America's largest mutual fund in the late 1990s. And when that transformative tech rally turned into a dot-com bubble, a new generation of superstars emerged. Forgive me if I can't remember their names.

My point is that portfolio management is a team sport. It's nice to have stars, but only if they help the team win consistently. That was the job of our manager researchers: to determine the impact of the investment stars on the bigger picture. At Russell, we analyzed that person's style to see whether it would mesh with that of the other players—whether it would work as part of a total portfolio that would control risk the way we wanted it to. If the answer was yes, then we'd hire the firm with the investment star—by all means. But we would watch that firm and that person very closely. If anything happened to change the status of that key individual, we would immediately put the product and, perhaps, the whole firm on our watch list.

Of course, we were also open to working with money management firms that function independently of any single individual. When a process is disciplined, tight, and well documented, replacing one experienced professional with another qualified individual is not a matter for concern.

And when we reach the level of the client's portfolio—the total portfolio with multiple asset classes, styles, and managers, we have effectively diversified the risk of overdependence on any individual. By definition, portfolio management is a team enterprise. When *value* is out of favor, *growth* steps up to carry the burden. Bonds diversify the risk of stocks, and vice versa. No security, sector, or asset class is perpetually the winner, but they all play a part. As a result, when you win, it's obvious that every member of the team gets a share of the credit. That's the nature of our industry; as such, I don't think it's a coincidence that sharing credit became so important in our culture.

The A Team

In previous chapters, I've talked about exemplary individuals and incidents that illustrate each element of the culture. However, when it comes to sharing credit, I find it tough to single out just a few. We had so many team players; just listing their names would take pages and pages.

Instead, I'm going to give just one example of a singular team effort—the design and construction of a new headquarters for Frank Russell Company at 909 A Street in Tacoma. And I will tell you about the unusual way we shared the credit after the project's completion.

We kept the company in The Rust Building through the late 1960s. It was a 12-story building; built in 1920, it had a 19th-century feel. My grandfather had used it all those years, and it had been adequate for our needs in the early days. Then we moved to the Washington Building, which at one time was billed as the second tallest building in the Pacific Northwest. It was another 1920s vintage structure, and we quickly outgrew it as the consulting practice began to take off.

We finally moved when we had the opportunity to rent space in the First Interstate Bank building in May 1973. It was a brand-new office tower, all concrete and glass, one of the tallest buildings in Tacoma. Our new location was just a few blocks away, but it felt like we were moving into the 20th century.

However, after 1980 our needs for space increased dramatically. Head count was growing rapidly as we gained traction in our data and investment management businesses. From a legal perspective, we needed to maintain distinct areas for each of the businesses. Obviously, we couldn't prevent the people from mingling at times. But the physical layout would remind customers and associates that the businesses were separate.

By the mid-1980s, the need for space became acute. There wasn't room to expand in the First Interstate Building. And there was nothing adequate anywhere in Tacoma. Finally, in 1985 we concluded it was time to build our own headquarters.

Now Wall Street has many colorful sayings. For example: *If you want a friend on Wall Street, get a dog.* It's an exaggeration, of course. But it does reflect a home truth that is part of the reason why we were happy to keep the company headquartered in the Pacific Northwest. I'm also aware of the adage that reminds investors to be wary when a fast-growing company decides to build an elaborate new headquarters—a monument to itself. I don't think you could fairly say that of the Russell building at 909 A Street in Tacoma. It was a big investment and those are always risky—by definition. But our decision was driven entirely by the numbers. We had outgrown the space we were currently occupying, and it was more cost effective, long term, to own a property than to rent one.

We had no one on staff with experience in architecture or construction, but were able to field a very capable team of generalists, headed by our jack-of-all-trades, John James, and my wife, Jane.

I chose John because he had successfully handled every challenge I threw at him. We hired him to manage mutual fund operations for Bondstock. Later, we promoted him to general administrative director and, after that, head of human resources. John knows how to get things done and, as always, he was open to taking on something completely new.

And I chose Jane because the building was going to have our family's name on the front door. Jane had impeccable taste and, of course, she had my complete trust. She embodied the spirit of the company and it was gratifying to me to see how she was able to instill so many elements of the Russell culture into the building.

Jane and John had complementary skills and roles, but between them they didn't have an ounce of experience in architecture or construction. For example, I remember one time when Jane was having trouble reading a blueprint. She called our friend, Ish McLaughlin, who had run a large construction firm in Pittsburgh, and found out exactly what she needed to know.

The building at 909 A Street took two years to build. It had 225,000 square feet on 12 floors plus underground parking. It had a climate-controlled room for our mainframe computer and the latest in telecommunications equipment. It was also probably the first office in Tacoma to provide workout facilities for employees. In addition, we had to deal with complex structural requirements because the building sits on the edge of a ridge overlooking Commencement Bay. Jane and John's team brought the project in on time and under budget.

They did a great job! Afterwards, I asked all of the 15 people who were involved to come up to our house and have dinner to celebrate. I said to Jane, "Would you please have them all sit in a circle and serve a glass of wine to get them relaxed before dinner is served?" She said, "Why are you going to do that?" And I replied, "Well, I'll show you . . . ."

After everyone had arrived, we sat down in a circle. I put a $20 bill on the floor in the middle and I said, "Now I want everyone to tell the story of the biggest mistake you made in the last two years—starting with John." I glanced around the room. At first there were startled, sad looks on people's faces and I was afraid I might have miscalculated the mood.

But John got things rolling and, by the time three or four people had told their mistakes, everybody in the group was enjoying themselves. We went all around the room and, at the end, I asked Jane, "Who gets the 20 dollars?"

"Everybody," she said. "You have to pay 20 dollars to each person."

I like the fact that we recognized that everyone makes mistakes. If we're able to admit those mistakes to our associates, it helps make the lessons of experience more concrete and makes it less likely they'll be repeated. And that's really a constructive thing to think about.

Our Biggest Mistake

Did I make mistakes at Russell? Yes, scores of them—untold numbers. But I don't write them down or keep track. Internally, we often criticize ourselves for missing the transition from defined benefit (DB) to defined contribution (DC), which is to say, for failing to build a model for employee investors in 401(k)-type retirement plans that would be as widely accepted as our multi-manager approach to pension fund management. In fact, we always believed that multi-asset, multi-style, multi manger diversification was the right solution for investors of all types and sizes, individual or institutional, DB or DC.

As DC plans rose to prominence along with the extended bull run of the 1980s, mutual fund companies such as Fidelity and Vanguard successfully combined star managers like Peter Lynch and John Neff with a bundled recordkeeping and employee-education solution, and effectively dominated the market.

At Russell, we still believed we had a superior investment solution. It's ironic, of course, because I started out selling mutual funds to pension funds such as LTV. My major breakthrough came when I realized that using multiple institutional managers was a better solution. Now, a dozen years later, we found the market ignoring the lessons of diversification, and moving toward big mutual fund families mostly due to the administrative convenience of the bundled solution!

Objectively, we probably should have admitted we'd made a mistake: Our share of the DC market was a humble percentage of that managed by the mutual giants. But correcting our error would have meant buying or developing DC plan administration capabilities. Would that have been the best use of our resources? Instead of copying the mutual fund companies' bundled approach, we decided to continue with our strategy of expanding globally.

I fired a shot across the market's bow, in the form of a speech entitled, "Parallel Worlds: How Plan Sponsors Can Put 30 Years of Defined Benefit Experience to Work in Their Defined Contribution Plans." I first delivered it at a *Pensions & Investments* conference in October 1998. My thesis was that DC plans were at serious risk of becoming a train wreck, if they didn't change their ways. Participants weren't saving enough or allocating assets properly to achieve the growth they'd need to retire. And plan sponsors weren't offering the right options to allow them to diversify properly. As I noted at the time,

> Using one mutual fund in each asset class is not the answer. Hiring a mutual fund family is, essentially, a single-manager hire—because of consistencies in philosophy and process from fund to fund. There is a strong parallel here to the

"balanced" approach plan sponsors used to take in hiring a single bank or insurance company to manage all of the pension assets. We got over that in the 70s.

I can't say that my speech changed the market. But 10 years later, government regulations have moved in our direction. Plan sponsors are allowed to provide advice and to automatically enroll participants in "qualified default investment options" that are diversified by asset class—rather than in some sort of cash equivalent. That is a step in the right direction. However, style and manager diversification are still missing. Maybe in another 10 years, they'll address that issue, too.

I feel good that we did the right thing. We stuck to our market position that plan sponsors needed to provide fully diversified funds so employees could properly protect their investments. But objectively, we had to admit that our share of the U.S. defined-contribution market share was small in comparison to our competitors'. Did we learn anything from that mistake? I'd argue that focusing on non-U.S. markets, particularly Europe, but also Australasia, was a smart strategy. We were late to the game in the U.S.; it was questionable whether we could ever catch up.

But we were able to recognize that most developed countries face the same retirement issues that we do in the U.S., but without the entrenched presence of mutual funds. We were able to get in early and establish strategic relationships with a great set of partners. Today, a significant percentage of Russell Investments' revenue comes from overseas. And we are well-positioned to compete going forward.

The bottom line is: The lessons you learn from your mistakes aren't always the obvious ones. Don't be too quick to change course when your errors are based on long-term strategies or deeply held principles.

Plenty to Celebrate

Of course, most mistakes are not strategic. They're just some variation on the theme of human error. These, you should try to acknowledge right away, make any needed corrections, and move on. We had plenty of examples of this type of mistake over the years.

One of the most notable occurred in 1973, when I was visiting our consulting clients as part of our regular review process and also to introduce Blake Eagle and the concept of diversification into real estate as an investable asset class. We arrived in St. Louis and handed out the portfolio reports. Upon opening them, the Monsanto people noted that the portfolios belonged to Caterpillar Corporation. The executives started giving me a hard time. "How are we going to discuss our portfolio with this set of data, George?" At least their tone was bantering, not hostile. I reached into my pocket and pulled out the tape recorder I always carried in those days. I began to dictate a memo to the admin staff back in Tacoma, so that everyone could hear. "In the future," I said, trying to sound calm, "please be certain to put the right stuff in the right place in my travel files." Then I clicked off the recorder and told the Monsanto people that we'd have their reports in their hands by the end of the following day. Before anyone could get up to leave, I added, "And we might as well look at these Cat files because elements of their strategy are also relevant to your situation."

Obviously, that was a major error, but we salvaged the situation by staying calm and showing the client that everything was under control. We had made an honest mistake and we would simply correct it. That gave Monsanto the confidence that we believed in our people, so we were able to retain their trust. And it didn't unnecessarily punish anyone. Everyone in the office knew we had made a mistake. Of course they felt terrible, but what could they do? I can assure you it never happened again. Monsanto remained a client and people on the admin team continued to help me personally and add value to the company for decades. At Russell, when there's a mistake, we march on and let it disappear. I don't keep a record in my mind.

Over the years, we've obviously hired some people who have not fit in well with the Russell culture. Back in the early 1970s, one of our senior associates declined to drop off a package at the airport, even though it was hardly out of his way. I told him that everybody in the company was expected to do whatever was necessary to get the job done—even washing windows. I think that was the only time I ever used profanity with an associate. And "window washing" became part of the vocabulary of many of the older hands in the company. It meant that everybody shares in the work, in the credit, and in the rewards.

By the time Mike Phillips took over as president and CEO, our culture had become both more mature and more refined. We had been through several business cycles, and we knew more about how to mentor our young associates.

One of these was Mark Castelin, a young research analyst that Madelyn had hired to help pioneer a new asset class: emerging markets. This was the wildest new investment frontier at that particular time, and Mark had the perfect personality for it. He was from Alaska and had just taken his MBA with a 4.0 grade point average. He was tough and smart—and he knew it.

A position had opened up in our London office, and Mark was one of the finalists. He made an appointment with Mike Phillips to talk to him about life in London. As it was a magnificent fall day, Mike suggested they take sack lunches over to Fireman's Park, right next door to the new Russell building, where they could enjoy the sunshine and the view of Commencement Bay and Mt. Rainier.

They sat down together, and Mike came straight to the point. "I know you want to talk about London," he said, "but I want to talk to you about something else. You've been at this company for maybe six months and you have a little bit of a reputation of being a Rambo. But you'll never be successful at Frank Russell Company by being a Rambo." Mike advised Mark to relax a bit and try to work more with people one on one.

Fortunately, Mark understood that this was an opportunity, not a rebuke. In his own words:

> Mike's advice really struck home for a number of reasons. Number one was the fact that my CEO, of all people, would have heard about somebody like me, who was fairly new

and junior in the company, and he had taken the time and trouble to develop an accurate insight into what was going on. That was really profound. Number two, it told me that Frank Russell Company really supported people in their own right—their growth and well-being. It was not just a matter of technical and professional proficiency, but becoming interpersonally proficient as well.

Mark took the lesson to heart and subsequently had a closed-door conversation with every single one of his colleagues in the international manager research group. Without exception, they took advantage of the opportunity to tell him, "Yes, you've been kind of a butt for the last six months." But it cleared the air. Mutual respect was established and the group could start moving forward as a team. In addition, Mark became an apostle for the Russell culture, because it helped him to "ground myself in how I deal with people throughout the organization, trying to promote a positive outcome for everybody." As Mark explains it, "You'll never see that in the P&L statements but, at an individual level, Russell culture is about helping one another grow, giving advice and helping your associates advance in their career paths. Hopefully, that is something that everyone at Russell can contribute to the next generation as they go through their careers here."

The key to this story is that Mike didn't attack Mark; he attacked "Rambo," because he could do that without destroying Mark's self-image. People need a healthy self-concept to be effective. But if you grind on people repeatedly about mistakes, they tend to get defensive. You don't want mistakes to linger and become a weight on people. If you're constantly making a big deal out of ordinary human error, your people will probably make mistakes more often than they would in a positive, supportive environment. People don't work well when they're always on the defensive. Particularly in competitive business situations, you need associates who are confident and can assume an offensive, can-do attitude. That's what is so inspiring about Mike Phillips' conversation with Mark Castelin. Because Mike took the time to be a mentor, he converted Mark into a team-player who could still bring an effective, competitive edge to his business responsibilities.

Sharing Credit—Globally

Mike Phillips is an incredibly skilled executive. In Chapter 8, "Plan Transitions," I'll explain in detail why I chose him as my successor. Right now, I simply wanted to observe that his singular British charm and tact made him particularly effective at bringing people together. His success at integrating Mark with the rest of the manager research team was not an isolated incident. Mike was responsible for the much larger, "global" challenge of unifying offices on four different continents into a single culture.

Managing growth is always a challenge, even when international boundaries are not involved. I know from experience. Growing from a dozen people on one floor, to a company that occupies several floors—even that presents a challenge. When people don't see each other every day, there's a chance for different practices and processes to develop. It may seem like a small thing at first, but it can become serious, so you have to keep your eye on it.

But when you have hundreds of people, speaking different languages and working in more than a dozen different locations around the world, it becomes a major challenge just to make it work.

For example, there's the issue of consistency. How do you make sure that something as qualitative as manager research is consistent and objective across asset classes—and across continents? Fortunately, we had brilliant people like Andy Turner and Don Ezra to turn loose on the problem. They solved it by analyzing the issues, documenting procedures in a rigorous and disciplined fashion and creating innovative ways of quantifying the qualitative, while still honoring the essential value and integrity of subjective findings.

In a way, technical challenges like that one are easier to manage than the organizational ones. Standardizing global manager research gave the teams in different parts of the world a compelling reason to work together. They got to know each other. They shared the setbacks and enjoyed the triumphs *together.*

Other functional areas took longer to integrate, particularly if they didn't have an urgent reason to work together. I once heard that the London-based marketing people were miffed with their counterparts in Tacoma. It seems that business papers in the UK are trimmed a bit longer than the standard U.S. size, so they couldn't use the brochures that the team in Tacoma had developed. A trivial issue, but symptomatic of people who are not ready to share credit.

Building rapport and team spirit in a global company is a huge challenge, because it takes time. The distances and other differences between London and Tacoma, or Tacoma and Tokyo— not to mention Tokyo and London—are enormous. It takes time for people to connect, to get to know each other, to learn what the value proposition is in Tacoma and then buy into it.

Fragmentation is an inevitable part of an international organization. You can eliminate a lot, but not all of it. The organizational structure and reporting relationships are complex. That's why it was important to have someone like Mike Phillips there to patiently bridge the gaps. Though he eventually took U.S. citizenship, Mike's identity as an Englishman helped gain the confidence of our international associates. It showed that you didn't have to be from Tacoma to attain the highest level in the company.

Sharing credit by delegating key management responsibilities is a powerful tool for uniting an organization.

Sharing Ownership

An even more powerful unifying force is sharing ownership in the company. Of course this is a common practice that has been around for a long time in public companies. Employee stock ownership plans are wonderful for getting employees to think like owners (as long as management doesn't use company stock, rather than cash, to match employee contributions to the retirement plan; then you don't get proper diversification!). Stock options were the fuel that drove the tech boom in the 1990s; likewise, they were the flotsam and jetsam of the post-bubble collapse. In any case, there's no doubt that ownership creates a strong alignment of interests between management and employees. By sharing ownership you motivate people to work harder and stay longer—all the things that enable a company to end up with a better net result. It's a partnership.

I have to confess that sharing ownership with associates was not my idea. Credit for that goes to Duncan Smith. It happened in late spring or summer of 1985. We'd been growing revenues at approximately 25 percent per annum for the past 10 years—since the market recovered from the deep recession of 1973–1974. So we were doing well, but profits were not all that visible because we continued to invest in growing our investment businesses, which did not even have a five-year track record as yet.

At that time, we were still in the First Interstate Building, and I had instituted a process of gathering all officers of Frank Russell Company so we could air our views and discuss the direction of the company. On this particular occasion, we were talking about plans for the coming year. I was presenting a slide that talked about motivating and retaining employees when Duncan raised his hand.

I should have known something remarkable was about to happen.

"When we research investment managers," Duncan said, "we place a relatively high importance on the key professionals having ownership in the firm. And is there any thought about a program for the key professionals in Frank Russell Company?"

I pointed to the slide where the topic was "motivation" and said, "That's what we're talking about. That's right here."

I guess Duncan thought I was being dense, so he spelled it out for me—literally. He grabbed a felt pen and wrote on the whiteboard, one letter at a time: *O-W-N-E-R-S-H-I-P.* Now some people are turned off by Duncan's flamboyant manner. But I'd learned to ignore the manner and focus on the content.

Next morning I had a surprise of my own prepared for Duncan. I asked him to come into my office and directed him to work on developing a phantom stock plan with some people I'd already contacted. So ownership was up and running. I think it safe to say that stock ownership has a stronger impact on people's performance than the word *motivation* on a presentation slide.

The original stock plan included about 250 people who were selected based on their ability to positively impact the company's performance. Over the years, we created other pools and broadened the participation criteria so that, eventually, we included every associate. By the time I sold Frank Russell Company to Northwestern Mutual in 1999, our associates owned approximately 40 percent of the stock. They deserved every penny: I may have founded the company, but I give associates full credit—then, and now—for helping to create the value that has continued to increase long after I stopped playing an active role.

Key Points from Chapter 6

1. You can't go it alone. Bringing people together and sharing credit with them will result in dramatic improvements in productivity.
2. Don't be afraid of hiring "stars" if you have the opportunity. Just make sure they have the team orientation to go with their professional talent.
3. Celebrating mistakes is the mirror image of sharing credit. It's almost like asset allocation, because the combination attenuates the extreme highs and lows. This practice keeps people on an even keel and better able to focus on the future.
4. Done right, pointing out mistakes is a form of mentoring—a powerful tool for helping people advance their careers.
5. Strategic business mistakes are different from everyday human error. The lessons are never obvious and require more time for evaluation.
6. With ordinary mistakes, say what needs to be said and then forget about it.
7. Sharing responsibility and ownership are the ultimate tools for sharing credit. Use them judiciously.

CHAPTER

Recognize Luck

"AND LEARN HOW TO BET ON YOUR INTUITION."

L uck has a much bigger role in business success than people generally care to admit. In my experience building Frank Russell Company, luck played an important role at many critical junctures.

As you'll recall, it was a chance meeting with Jim Ling's assistant that enabled me to make my first big mutual fund sale to a pension fund. Then, when I realized that pension funds were actually looking for help in selecting managers, I was extremely lucky to reach Paul Kaltinick on my first cold call. At that time, almost anyone else in the industry probably would have turned me down flat. If that had happened, I suppose I would have then moved along to the next CFO's name on the next S&P sheet. But when you're excited about a new idea, if you call four or five people in a row and they all turn you down, you tend to lose your enthusiasm. That was an exceptional piece of good luck to get a positive response on the first call.

Similarly, my brash promise to Pennsylvania Railroad, "We use the Dietz Method," proved to be prophetic, and that was a major stroke of luck as my intuition was several steps ahead of reality on that one.

And our high-stakes entry into the investment management business resulted from my—choose the term you like best—instinctive, impulsive, intuition-based response to Burlington Industries' question about how to apply our multi-manager strategy to a small subsidiary.

A lot of people hold the opinion that "you make your breaks." They view luck mostly as the outcome of hard work and preparation. Thomas Edison is the standard-bearer for this view. Everybody knows his aphorism: "Genius is one percent inspiration and 99 percent perspiration." And, if that wasn't clear enough, he explained: "I never did anything worth doing by accident, nor did any of my inventions come by accident. They came by work."

But all of us know plenty of people who work hard, yet never get lucky. They never seem to get their one percent of inspiration—if that's the right number. Possibly, they are so focused on working hard, they don't mind all of that perspiration or the fact that it may be clouding their vision. And the critical moment passes without their realizing it.

For example, I had been working extremely hard at building my mutual fund business for 11 years when I met Jim Ling's assistant. Making a big sale to a pension fund was the break *I'd* been looking for. But the lucky part wasn't the transaction itself; it was the opportunity to meet people who were in charge of large pension funds, and to understand what *the market* was looking for.

When I called JCPenney, I actually wanted to talk to the person named on the S&P sheet, who happened to be the chief financial officer. As a hardworking salesperson, I could have easily passed on the opportunity to talk to Paul Kaltinick, because he was not the decision maker I thought I needed to reach.

And when Burlington Industries inquired about their subsidiary, there were any number of responsible, hardworking, businesslike responses I could have made: "That's outside our core focus." "It might be a conflict of interest." "We'll have to study it because it would require a substantial investment of time and money."

I'm sure you can see where I'm heading with this. I reject the notion that luck is just hard work in disguise. Perhaps hard work does put you in a position where you can meet people like Jim Ling's assistant or Paul Kaltinick. But then you have to recognize the opportunity when it presents itself. I'd put it this way: The lucky break is always something different from what you were expecting or working for. *The trick is being able to recognize luck and respond decisively.* That takes a positive attitude in general, plus an openness to new opportunities that you haven't anticipated.

Are You a Decision Maker?

I think intuitive decision making came to me naturally. For as long as I can remember, my practice has been to get the facts and then "just do it." I'm comfortable with the idea that I will never have *all of the information* I'd like to have under ideal circumstances in order to make a decision. Instead, my goal is to collect *enough information* to make a decision in the time available. That's why it's called "risk taking," because you never have 100 percent certainty. You have to accept that fact or you'll never be able to make a decision at a critical time.

But not everyone thinks or operates this way. I ran across a very interesting contrast several years ago at the Monterey Institute of International Studies. The National Bureau of Asian Research was hosting a two-day conference there and I was the dinner speaker at the end of the first day.

The conference organizers told me it was the largest group of China experts ever assembled in one room at the same time. During the first day, I must have listened to eight or nine hours of presentations. I remember thinking, "This is scary." Without exception, each person was articulate and authoritative. Even in the Q&A, the presenters could take 15 minutes to answer a single question, peppering their response with all of the salient facts, details, and references. They truly seemed to possess *all* of the knowledge that you could ever want. I suppose I felt intimidated, because the topic I'd chosen to discuss at dinner was simply: How do you invest in developing Asia?

Just before I got to the podium it occurred to me what was going on, and I had just enough time to formulate it as a good news/bad news vignette. "The good news," I said, "is that I learned a lot, and it was terrific to be with you. The bad news is that if I'd been with you for the past 10 years I would never have made an investment into developing Asia."

Of course I had to explain that.

"As an academic," I said, "your job is to debate an issue on all sides, and there is no end in sight for the debate because you don't ever have to make a decision. But anybody in this room who is running a business needs to stop collecting facts at a certain point and make a decision."

This went over surprisingly well. On the next day, I counted at least a dozen positive references to my remarks. This suggests that decision making is a skill that can be acquired—even later in life—under the right circumstances. First, you need to approach the problem with a decision-making mindset. And culture has a big influence. I had fun teasing my academic colleagues about their lack of decision-making prowess. But in all fairness, that's what the academic life is all about—debate, discussions, publications, and then more debate. Academics aren't expected to make decisions—just the opposite. So the outcome is not surprising.

What about business culture? As I pointed out at the conference, business success requires sound decisions. But that does not mean that individual businesses or businesspeople have good decision-making processes. In fact, I included "Recognize luck—and learn how to bet on your intuition" as part of the Russell culture precisely because effective decision making was an area where we always needed improvement.

The Decision Factory

We refer to investment management as an industry, but I wonder how many people have thought carefully about the nature of the output this "industry" produces. I think one of our long-time associates, Jeff Hansen, nailed it when he said, "Investment firms are essentially pure decision-making organizations." That's an important insight, which first appeared in a book Jeff wrote about entrepreneurial decision making, called *Growth and Change Made Easy*.[1] Jeff worked in a variety of roles at Russell, including research analyst, head of consulting in Japan, and finally, director of management consulting. After countless hours of interviews with money managers, Jeff came to a simple realization: All of the training that portfolio managers receive, all of the research, and all of the resources of the multitrillion-dollar investment industry are focused on making one basic decision: *buy, sell, or hold*.

At Russell, our job was to study these decision-making machines. We wanted to find out what made them tick. But ultimately, what our clients cared about was our ability to recommend the ones that would make money for them in the future. So even though we knew a lot about decision making, our real job was making decisions ourselves. That's not so easy when there's money on the line—not just your future fees, but also your client's ability to pay pension liabilities. In the broadest context, if you make the right decision, then thousands or millions of people get to have a financially secure retirement. If not, then life gets considerably more complicated. Those are the stakes.

How do you deal with that level of responsibility? Personally, I would have been paralyzed if I'd spent too much time trying to overthink it. I always tried to do just the right amount of research and then go with my gut feeling. Then, of course, I'd deal with the consequences, good or bad.

I noticed over time that external events tend to have their own direction; they pick their own course. Like it or not, that's the way you're going, so you adjust to the circumstances. For example, you may have planned to make a particular decision by the end of the year. Then something happens on December 1, and the decision has to be made without delay. There's no choice. You must move forward much sooner than you'd planned. All you can do is make the decision and then manage the risks. If you're in a leadership position, this is something you're going to have to do on a regular basis. I don't know that it's a skill; I think it's more of an automatic response mechanism. I compare it to steering a boat through a rough sea with green water coming over the bow. You're pitching forward until it feels like you're nearly vertical. The sea only gets bigger. You have to rely on your intuitive reactions—how to steer, when to slow down, when to speed up. If that's too dramatic, think of driving a car in city traffic, or raising children. There's no time to stop and read a book or ask for an outside opinion. You just have to decide—yes or no, left or right, stop or go.

Decision Triggers

I've always been comfortable moving forward. I'd much rather live that way than just wait and wait and never make a decision. But as the organization grew, we had to formalize our decision-making processes. In the early 1970s, when Madelyn Smith first started researching managers, we had an assignment for the endowment board of a major local university. They had $15 million that they wanted to place with an equity fund in Seattle. I gave Madelyn the names of three likely candidates, and told her to get to work.

Madelyn did that. It was no problem. She interviewed the three firms and wrote up a qualitative assessment of each one. I looked it over. It was good work. Then I said, "Okay, Madelyn, which one should get the $15 million?"

She tried to plead inexperience. "I'm too new at this. I am giving you the pros and cons of each firm, but I really can't make that decision."

I told her that was fine. And I gathered my papers to leave. Then, on impulse, I said, "Madelyn, just imagine I gave you a million dollars right now and told you that it had to be managed by one of those firms in Seattle—which one would you give your million to?"

The idea that it was her money—not the endowment's—enabled her to bypass all of her reservations. "There's no question in my mind; I really liked that startup firm, even though they've only been open for a few months." The next day, I wrote a letter to the endowment board forwarding Madelyn's recommendation.

But that's not the end of the story. In the ensuing years, when Madelyn became director of equity research, she'd use the same technique to train new generations of manager researchers; this was a group with exceptional analytical skills, who, like Madelyn herself, happened to need a bit of help when it came time to make the actual recommendation. In that situation, Madelyn would say, "I just gave you a million dollars: Would you leave it with the current manager or hire someone else?" It seemed to clarify their thinking immediately. It's fascinating how a simple, transparent device, like pretending it's your money instead of the client's, can free the mind to make decisions.

Sometimes, it's not a fictional device, but an unexpected question that forces you to think about things in a new context. When Burlington Industries asked me about their subsidiary, I remember needing a moment of silence. Then the answer appeared—not quite fully formed, but with most of the essential elements roughed in.

And I suppose I was trying to emulate or repeat that moment of inspiration with the legal teams that I'd hired to work out the details of creating our manager of manager trust funds. Somehow, the fiction that my car keys were the keys to the restroom helped them to resolve a complex legal problem in a matter of hours.

Intuition is so powerful, it can seem almost magical when you find ways to unleash it. Obviously, in the normal course of business I couldn't go around jingling my car keys all of the time. But I would go out of my way to talk to associates about using intuition. I also kept meetings extremely short; that was partly due to the requirements of my schedule, but also to encourage associates to do more with less talk—to encourage more intuitive decision making. I once sent a company-wide memo suggesting that, as the conference room chairs were wearing out more quickly than expected, perhaps it would be better not to replace them. Some people actually thought I was joking.

We also encouraged innovative thinking and did little or nothing to discourage entrepreneurial detours. Exploring dark alleys was definitely part of the culture. These explorations didn't always bear fruit; but when they did, the results could be sensational.

For example, we developed our next-generation asset allocation model in response to a more-or-less casual question—*Is it possible to do this?*—from one of our clients in Japan. I'm going to tell the story in detail in Chapter 9, because it's mostly about the necessity to keep taking risks. But a big part of the risk taking was the team's ability to use and rely on intuition as part of the product development process. Team leader Andy Turner recalls that, after Yasuda accepted our proposal, the team developed a visual rendition of our plan. As Andy recalls:

> It shows a bunch of steps at the start of the project and a couple of steps at the end. In the middle, there is this big sort of fuzzy ball and it says *A miracle occurs*. That was basically our project plan. We knew immediately some things we had to do, and then, after we solved the problem, what we were going to do. But we didn't have any idea how we were going to solve the problem in the middle. We just were trusting that we could do it.

I like that—planning to use your intuition just when you know you're going to need it!

Kelly Haughton Builds a Better Benchmark

As you can imagine, Russell culture was tough on our accountants, who had trouble measuring the contributions of luck, intuition, and miracles to the bottom line. That's why I want to tell the story of the Russell Indexes in detail, because it so clearly illustrates how intangibles—things that cannot be measured—can nevertheless contribute significant value to a business enterprise.

The story begins one day about 25 years ago. I was working in my office, when one of our young consultants knocked on my door. It was Kelly Haughton. He didn't have an appointment, but he said he needed to talk to me right away.

I motioned for him to come in. I work standing up, so I didn't need to get up. Kelly seemed agitated, so I just waited for him to tell me what was on his mind. He said, "What if Frank Russell Company could offer its clients a benchmark that is better than the S&P 500? What would you say to that?"

I thought it was a theoretical question, so I replied, "I'd say that I would need to see the printouts. It would need a lot of documentation."

Without missing a beat, Kelly said, "I've got it all right here." He stepped out of the office and came back a second later with a cart piled high with data printouts.

That was one of the biggest and best surprises I've had in my career. I didn't know this project even existed—and suddenly it lands on my doorstep, complete in almost every detail and ready for clients to use.

At the time, we knew that Kelly and his team had created an important tool for our consulting practice. Our manager research analysts had been frustrated for some time, because many managers' portfolios simply did not look like the S&P 500. Now we had a solution.

What we did not, and could not, foresee was how important the Russell Indexes would become to the public's perception of the company. Even today, if I'm in some part of the world, or even in the United States, where people don't know what I did professionally, I can most efficiently introduce myself by saying, "Are you familiar with the stock market index called the Russell 2000?"

They almost always say, "Yes, of course." Then I simply raise my hand and say, "I'm Russell."

The other outcome that we didn't expect was what a money-maker the Indexes would become. None of us predicted the phenomenal growth of passive investment strategies—we still believe in active management!—but as of 2009 there is $4.4 *trillion* benchmarked to the Russell Indexes. As Kelly likes to say, "In Tacoma, that's a lot of money." The Indexes also generate substantial revenue in the form of royalties.

GM Starts with a Clean Slate

Before joining Russell, Kelly had worked for Wells Fargo/Barclays Global Investors in the San Francisco Bay Area. Barclays is known as one of the top "quant" shops in the world. Fortunately for us, Kelly and his wife were yearning for a simpler lifestyle: Kelly called Peter Dietz. Peter recognized Kelly's talent and hired him in May 1981. Probably because of his quantitative background, I used to say to Kelly, "Go with your gut. We don't do that enough around here." It was pretty good advice, as it turned out.

In 1982, we signed up General Motors as a new client. This completed the "Triple Crown" of pension consulting for us, because at the time, AT&T, General Motors, and IBM had the three largest corporate pension funds in the U.S. Our initial project for GM was to create a massive report, analyzing every aspect of their plan. Ron Sellers led the project, with Joan Sobba, Kelly, and many others contributing their time and talents.

The legendary Gordon Binns had just taken over responsibility for GM's pension fund. Gordon showed his visionary character right away by challenging us to imagine that GM's equity program was a blank slate. They'd sold everything—now, how would we invest the cash? That got everybody's blood flowing. We had the tools we needed: a broad selection of managers whom we had researched qualitatively, the industry's best asset allocation model, our equity profile and attribution model, style analysis, and a dream team of experienced consultants. Our goal was to exceed client expectations—and now we had a client whose expectations were sky high.

Crossing the Threshold

When Kelly started thinking about the equity strategy for GM, the first thing that crossed his mind was the benchmark. People at Russell had been chafing at the shortcomings of the S&P 500 for some time. We felt that 500 stocks was an arbitrary number; the stocks included were selected by a committee at Standard & Poor's—and nobody knew what criteria they were using. As Kelly puts it, "To me it seemed more like an actively managed portfolio than a passive index." That's why he decided to consider the Wilshire 5000, which purported to represent the whole market.

Kelly wandered down the hall to discuss the idea of using the Wilshire 5000 with Madelyn Smith, who at that time was head of equity research. Madelyn's gut feeling was that the 5000 wouldn't work, but she asked to see an analytical profile on it. As it turned out, Kelly couldn't secure that information. Madelyn replied, "Well, we can't recommend an index when we don't even know what it looks like. . . ." So he was back to square one.

Now comes the moment we see depicted in every great story, starting with the *Iliad* when Achilles finally puts on his armor and comes out to fight, and continuing through the latest Bruce Willis movie; in a business context you might call it the *entrepreneurial moment.* I hope all of you reading this book will be as ready to respond to your entrepreneurial moment as Kelly was when he said to himself, "If I want a better benchmark I'm going to have to build it myself."

He started by trying to determine how many stocks to include in the benchmark. Kelly knew that many of the smallest stocks in the Wilshire 5000 were essentially illiquid and, in any case, too small for an institutional manager to buy without becoming a majority shareholder. The logical approach would be to limit the index's holdings to companies that managers could actually invest in. To determine that number, Kelly called colleagues around the industry who managed index funds. Their answers were consistent: They could invest in 3,000 to 3,200 stocks.

Kelly then decided to eliminate non-U.S. companies that were listed on U.S. exchanges—Royal Dutch/Shell, for example. In 1982, many Russell clients were already diversifying their portfolios with international equities, so it was important to have a benchmark that purely represented the performance of U.S. stocks. That brought the number down to 3,000.

Kelly did the work to compile the list of 3,000 names and, again, took the result to Madelyn. In Kelly's own words, here's what happened next:

> I said, "Okay, Madelyn, we've got the Russell 3000, but we probably need to subdivide it because we have money managers who specialize in particular aspects of the market. Do you want us to create the top 500?" And Madelyn said, "No; large-cap managers tend to specialize in about the top 1000 companies, not the top 500." So that was Madelyn's intuition. Our large-cap benchmark became the Russell 1000, and the Russell 2000 was just what was left over. It's ironic that, today, our leftover index, the Russell 2000, has become our most famous index.

Testing the Concept

This is where the story gets interesting. Remember that cart piled high with data? That was Kelly's next challenge—and it didn't come easily.

Madelyn was completely on board with the concept of the family of Indexes. But, once again, she said she needed formal documentation of all of the equity characteristics, plus five years of performance history. This meant that Kelly had to get a lot of help and computer access in order to produce it.

To complicate matters, several of Kelly's managers stepped in at this point and told him to stop working on the Indexes. In fact, they had to tell him repeatedly because Kelly kept ignoring them (rank insubordination, of course).

Kelly's solution was to go underground. Because mainframe computer time was still at a premium, Kelly recruited two of our IT people to his skunkworks, Judy Adams and Hank Hendrickson, and they secretly worked on the data in the dark of night and on weekends. When they finally finished, Kelly put the data on a cart and brought it upstairs for me to inspect.

The Russell Indexes became popular with our clients right away. They immediately saw the value of objectivity, consistency, and transparency in their equity benchmarks. But commercial success was still a long way in the future. We started to get excited in 1993, when the *Wall Street Journal* changed its longtime practice of running two articles on stocks every day, one focused on the NYSE and the other on NASDAQ. One of our PR people convinced them that this was an arbitrary distinction, as there were many gigantic companies on NASDAQ, such as Microsoft, Cisco, and Intel. As a result, the *Journal* changed the two columns' focus to large stocks and small stocks and began citing our Indexes.

Next, as the tech bubble began inflating in 1995, we were pleased to see our Index returns floating by on the tickers of the many new investing shows cropping up on the cable networks.

Today, we're proud of the fact that inclusion in the Russell 3000 is now the recognized sign that a company has come of age. In the old days, entrepreneurs at small public companies had to wait until one of the big brokerage houses initiated coverage.

Despite the visibility of the Indexes, for much of their history they were not a source of revenue for the company. I used to joke about it. I used to call the Indexes "the only product we don't make any money on."

All of that changed in the past 10 years. As I mentioned earlier, the revenues from licensing fees today make the Russell Indexes the company's second most profitable line of business. And all of this happened without conscious planning or foresight.

I do think it's accurate to say that the Indexes were a natural evolution of the Russell culture: We had hired, opportunistically, a very smart person, Kelly Haughton, who wanted to do the right thing for our clients. We encouraged him to use his intuition, and to work as part of a team—albeit a secret one—and this fabulous creation, the Russell Indexes, was the result. Though they were not profitable for more than a decade, we were patient, we persisted—and at last, through a stroke of good luck, we finally reaped a financial reward as market demand turned our Indexes into a highly profitable enterprise.

How Much is Luck and How Much is Skill?

When we research managers, one of our fundamental questions about their performance is, "How much is luck and how much is skill?" For example, suppose a manager was able to beat the Russell 1000 Index by 500 basis points in a given year. That's a great result. But then we would look more closely. What style does the manager use? If growth, then we'd look at the Russell 1000 Growth Index, because it's a better benchmark, a more relevant comparison. Now we see that the manager's outperformance is "only" 50 basis points. So, on our first pass we'd say this looks like a good professional growth manager, with 50 basis points attributable to skill and the rest to the market or style—in other words, to good luck.

In reviewing the history of Frank Russell Company, it seems fair to ask the same question: How much of our success is attributable to luck and how much to skill? The time frame during which I led Frank Russell Company basically corresponds to the last three decades of the 20th century. This was a great time to be an investor. If you look at the stock chart for the entire century, you see that stocks finally recover from the 1930s Depression in 1982 and that the trend after that is an almost unrelentingly upward slope. Obviously, it was a good time to be in the investment business.

A second key trend is harder to describe. Some would simply call it the passage of the Employee Retirement Income Security Act (ERISA) in 1974. I talked quite a bit about ERISA in Chapter 2. It's the legislation that established the basic definitions of fiduciary responsibility, and it meant that retirement plans had to either have trained professionals on staff or else hire consultants who could provide the needed expertise.

While the legislation's passage was important, I would say it was an event or a data point in a larger trend that I'd call the *professionalization* of the investment industry. That's what we were doing in 1969—bringing professional rigor, objective standards, and new technology to the management of retirement assets. And we weren't alone. We needed professional managers like Capital Group and Batterymarch. And we needed CFOs and treasurers like Paul Kaltinick at JCPenney, Bob Angelica and Dave Feldman at AT&T, and Adrian Cassidy at Pacific Telephone, who wanted to raise standards for managing pension money within their organizations.

None of us knew ERISA was coming; we welcomed it when it passed, because it just made our concept that much stronger. By 1974, we already had our 40 clients, so it didn't bring us new business. But remember how, at the beginning, Paul Kaltinick wasn't sure that he needed us after we had made our initial manager recommendations? The passage of ERISA helped to affirm the decision on the client's part that the consulting relationship was going to be an ongoing one, rather than a one-year engagement.

The professionalization of the industry continued to march forward after ERISA. When GM hired us in 1982, they already had a highly professional, sophisticated staff headed by Gordon Binns; they had developed sophisticated software on their own; and their needs for a consultant had evolved far beyond the simple manager searches we'd been doing only a decade earlier. Fortunately, we'd been part of this trend from the beginning and had certainly kept pace—often setting it—as the industry developed.

To return to the question of luck or skill: If you're willing to give Frank Russell Company a score similar to that of our fictional growth manager—500 basis points of outperformance— then I'd say, off the top of my head, that 50 of those basis points were attributable to skill and the rest to the market and/or good luck. Ultimately, the company's legacy will rest on a much broader set of measures than just financial performance. These include our ability to continue to provide productive employment for our associates; the way we interact with and support our community; and most importantly, the degree to which we are successful in achieving our mission of improving financial security for people.

As I write this chapter at the end of 2008, we are experiencing a market downturn that is as severe as anything we've experienced in a generation. Well-known financial institutions have gone bankrupt; investment strategies that were touted as risk management tools have failed; and the value of securities has declined in virtually every market globally, in every asset class. This is typical of a panic. Investors flee the market—all markets—indiscriminately, and this is a risk that cannot be diversified.

The antidote to a panic is patience. Markets will regain their equilibrium when people become calm enough to see that goods and services are still being produced, and still have value that other people are willing to pay for. That said, the enormous post-World War II generation has unquestionably suffered a major setback as it prepares for retirement. Will our company's, and the industry's, resources be adequate to the task of making up this lost ground? I believe they will, but it will require some strong intuitive thinking, a healthy dose of good luck, and possibly a minor miracle or two. These are rough seas, but we've weathered them before. We've always found a way.

A Grammatical Postscript

Many people have wondered why we call our benchmarks *indexes* rather than *indices*. Many of us were taught in grade school that you form the plural of Latin words by changing the *ex* ending to *ices*. We have heard the undignified sniggering over the years, from people who imagine we don't know our grammar.

In fact, credit for Americanizing *indices* to *indexes* goes to Joan Sobba. She argued that *indexes* would differentiate Russell from run-of-the-mill providers of *indices*. I found this persuasive, particularly in light of the precedent set by the leaders of Kimberly-Clarke Corporation, who wisely refrained from forming the plural of "Kleenex" as "Kleenices."

Note

1. Jeffrey A. Hansen, *Growth and Change Made Easy* (New York: Entrepreneur Press, 2005).

Key Points from Chapter 7

1. Luck is never what you expect. Recognizing luck requires a willingness to deviate from plans and entertain possibilities no one could have anticipated.
2. To be a successful decision maker, you must first be predisposed to make decisions. Many people are, by education and training, comfortable with endless research and discussion, but not decision making. From a business perspective, "more research" is nothing but procrastination.
3. Intuitive decision making is a characteristic shared by parents, drivers, captains of vessels at sea, and businesspeople. Forces of nature and complex human systems demand instantaneous decisions—and they'd better be the right ones!
4. *Decision triggers* are devices such as fictional scenarios or unexpected questions that can help people make intuitive decisions. Try using them on yourself, as well as with others in your organization.
5. Intuition alone may not be enough. However, if you hire smart people who are trying to do the right thing; if you give them the leeway to be creative and use their intuition; and if you are patient enough to wait longer than a few months or a few quarters, spectacular results might occur.

CHAPTER

Plan Transitions

"HIRE YOUR REPLACEMENT."

The following is a true story:

One morning in 1989, a group of Frank Russell Company executives convened for their monthly meeting. It was an unusual situation because the company founder, owner, and chief executive was out of town with his wife on an extended trip. Of course the executives on the committee were all capable: Any one of them could easily have chaired the meeting. But there was an unprecedented agenda item that they had to tackle first.

There was a sealed letter from their leader, George Russell. It was written on company stationery, and there was no postage or address—just instructions to read it at the beginning of the meeting. Apparently, it had been written before he and Jane had left on their trip.

Michael Phillips, global director of Frank Russell Company's consulting division, quickly scanned the letter. "It's from George," he said. "No surprise there. But listen to this . . . ," and he began to read aloud. There were only a couple of lines:

> *Jane and I have gone down in an airplane accident. What are you going to do about it?*
>
> *George*
>
> *P.S. If I make it back, I would like to read the minutes.*

In addition to the note, there was a sheaf of papers that turned out to be extracts of the wills of George and Jane Russell. The executives stood up and leaned in to get a better view of the documents. They included Lynn Anderson, CEO of the investment business, Marty Ryan, who was in charge of the data division, Jan Twardowski, who headed FRS (Frank Russell Securities), Jim McDonald, the CFO, and possibly one or two others.

Michael Phillips correctly sized up the situation; he knew exactly what the group needed to do right away. He said, "The first thing we have to do is to select a new leader, because I'm telling you, if George sees these minutes and we haven't selected a leader in the first half hour, we're going to get dinged."

Lynn Anderson said, "Well, I agree and I think that the leader should be Mike."

Mike tried to open the floor to other possibilities. "Look, I didn't make that statement because I wanted to be the leader. I don't really care who the leader is; we'd just better make sure we get a leader. Because if we don't, I know George is going to give us a tough time."

Everybody agreed with that—as far as it went: They weren't going to let Mike Phillips off the hook. They gave him the chair and said, "Okay, you're the leader."

And that's how I designated my successor.

Hire and Train Your Replacement

Actually, the process had begun several years earlier. I was celebrating my 50th birthday by climbing Mt. Rainier. At some point on the way to the summit, it occurred to me that I could fall into a crevasse; if that were to happen, it would be better for the company if I had a succession plan in place.

I picked one of our most promising executives and put him into a key position. It didn't work out and, a year later, I went to him and said, "I am awfully sorry: It's like taking the best player on the team and putting him in as coach. It only works occasionally." I told him he could leave if he wanted, but I'd prefer it if he stayed with the company. He stayed. He's doing great things; he's just not the coach.

Four years later, I tried again, but the same thing happened. I was beginning to get anxious—thinking I was down to my third strike. In addition, I was starting to become aware of tax issues that would come into play if Jane and I died while still owning the company. That's why I included the extracts of our wills as part of the succession-planning exercise for the executive committee. Not only did we need to choose the next CEO, but we also had to start preparing for the day we would sell Frank Russell Company.

I was looking for someone with specific qualities. First and foremost was non-negotiable integrity. I also wanted somebody with the ability to move fast when it came to making decisions. Liking change and the ability to adapt was another key characteristic, along with a temperament capable of ignoring the bottom line. Someone like that is not easy to find among today's professionally trained executives. Finally, it had to be someone who had earned internal support and would be readily accepted by his peers within the company. He had to be respected, supported, liked, and trusted.

The person who immediately came to mind was Michael Phillips. Jan Twardowski had hired Mike in December 1981. We had a principle in place throughout the company that gave our people the flexibility to change assignments—once they had hired and trained a suitable replacement. Although our London office was still small, we knew it was a strategic post. By the time Jan told me that he and his wife were ready to come home after four years in Europe, we agreed that Mike was an exceptional talent and would make an ideal replacement.

Mike had quite a cosmopolitan upbringing, as his father had been an ambassador and his family had spent considerable time in India and several other countries as well. Mike has a deft way of dealing with people; at the same time, he is a take-charge kind of guy. As Jan relates:

> On his first day I brought him along on a client meeting with Rank Xerox. What transpired at the meeting has become somewhat legendary. An hour into the meeting, the client asked some kind of investment strategy question, and I answered.
>
> Mike said, "Well you know, Jan, actually I would take a different approach." He then completely contradicted me, but in the nicest, most diplomatic way possible, so the client barely noticed. From that point on, they started focusing on him, and he kind of took over the meeting. Rank Xerox rapidly became his client. And then, of course, I made him my successor, so he took over my job in the London office. And a few years later, he took over my positions as head of international and then head of consulting. Those were very positive events for all of us, of course. He became a terrific boss and a great personal friend. But he started early in assuming leadership!

In January 1986, we brought Mike Phillips to Tacoma and gave him an important job: *director of consulting*. I told Jane, and nobody else, that I thought he was the person who would replace me. By 1989, I felt sure of the fact, but I needed to find out how Mike would be viewed by others in senior management, so I had that letter delivered to the executive committee.

The committee served as a senior brain trust that I depended on for high-level recommendations about the strategic direction of the company. I rarely, if ever, had to veto their advice. We were a team working together and it wasn't hard to come to conclusions that we all agreed to. People ask me from time to time, "What if they had come up with a different name, a different person?"

and invariably I look at them and just say, "Don't ask me questions that I don't have to answer."

The Apprenticeship of Michael Phillips

I announced my decision at the annual meeting in 1989, and Michael Phillips took over the job as president of Frank Russell Company in 1990.

If you ever find yourself in the position to appoint a successor, keep in mind that the person who has the qualifications to replace you is, by definition, overqualified to carry on for any length of time as your subordinate. At the same time, there are certain subtleties of the CEO job that you might wish to impart. You might think of it as a master class, where the outgoing maestro imparts a few remaining virtuoso flourishes to his already highly accomplished apprentice.

There is inherent tension in a relationship of this type, and Mike often used humor to keep things running smoothly. In his own words:

> I think a successful transition has to be based on mutual respect and non-dependence. In other words, you have to stay your own man. That was the way it worked with George and me. I used to kid him: When he showed me my office up on the 12th floor, it had been a conference room with a door that went out onto the gravel-covered roof. When George first showed it to me he said, "Well, Mike, now that you're going to be president, I want you to have this office. What do you think of it?"
>
> It was a very big office, and I think he was expecting me to be extremely appreciative. Instead, I said, "Well, George, it's okay as far as it goes." I gestured toward the door leading to my austere patio area covered with gravel. "Where are the pavers," I said, "where's the hot tub, where's the Cinzano umbrella, where's the wet bar?" George just looked at me with that gimlet stare he sometimes gets, and he said, "That's the wrong attitude."

I wasn't testing Mike. I knew he could do the job. But I wanted him to evolve into the role, instead of having an instant change of leadership. My philosophy is "walk, don't run," and it's really for the sake of all of the other people in the organization. I believed that in an abrupt transition, all the people that used to report to me might feel dislocated if they suddenly found themselves reporting to a different manager. By doing it slowly, we allowed the people who were close to me to develop relationships with Mike before he totally took charge. Ideally, the change is hardly recognizable from the outside, and I like that kind of transition process.

Even when you take a leadership succession at the right pace, it's hard to find the time to do the actual work of handing over your authority. The daily press of business is such that a lot of it has to happen automatically. The one exception was when I was traveling. As I mention in Chapter 5, "Work Hard," road trips were always occasions when I had more time I could use in a focused way. Traveling with Mike was probably the most successful element of our master class together. Since it's Mike's opinion that counts here, I'll let him tell it in his own words:

> Some of our most productive time together was when we were on the road. In Tacoma, George was always like a cat with five tails. He was always very, very busy going from one meeting to the other, so our meetings would be relatively short. But then he would take me on the road on one of his do-or-die, incredibly intense client trips and he would introduce me as his successor. So we would go around the country together and it was on those trips that we could have a really good interaction and talk about his views on our roles and the division of responsibilities.

By 1992, I felt that the foundation was in place—internally with associates and externally with clients—for Mike to take his place as CEO. I offered him the position. But he turned me down. He told me straight out that he didn't think I was ready to give up control. Mike said, "If *I* run the company, it means *you're* not going to run the company and you're not ready for that. We would clash and you would fire me."

I could see that Mike had a point. As founder of the company and owner of a controlling interest, I would be in an extremely influential position as chairman of the board. From my perspective, I had done a good job of delegating responsibility to Mike. I felt my remaining contribution would be that of an elder statesman who would indicate the strategic direction of the company in broad strokes, leaving Mike to run Frank Russell Company as he saw fit. It was clear to me that his talents in areas such as administration and negotiation with strategic partners already surpassed my own by a wide margin. I believed we had achieved the proper balance.

But, by declining my offer, Mike had made it clear that he had a different point of view. Since a "barely noticeable" transition was my objective, I didn't mind taking the extra time to think things over. Mike was doing an excellent job of running the company as president. And I was beginning to develop an interest in international relations and direct investments in emerging markets. I don't want to digress from the transition story to describe them in detail here; I'll save that for the next chapter, "Take Risks." Suffice it to say, these new ventures allowed me to play on the edges of the envelope and give Mike the breathing room he felt he needed. I went to him about a year after extending that first offer and said, "I'm ready now." It was 1993, and this time Mike agreed to accept the role of CEO of Frank Russell Company.

Mike Takes the Helm

The mid-to-late 1990s was a time of exuberant growth. Led by the technology sector and the liberalization of long-dormant markets like India and China, stock markets boomed around the world. While this trend was good for the investment management industry, it also spurred a proliferation of competitors.

You had to have the right strategy to succeed. With Mike at the helm, Frank Russell Company did an excellent job of growing clients' wealth while controlling risk. He extended the M-cubed investment model to more investors in the United States and around the world by extending our distribution through compatible partners. And the company prospered as a result.

Some of Mike's first big initiatives were directed internally. He needed to establish uniform standards, practices, and procedures across our global offices. He did this by inviting about a dozen of the company's key leaders to a retreat in Port Ludlow, which sits on the northern end of Puget Sound on the Olympic Peninsula. This meeting laid the foundation for making all of our investment management and manager research efforts a united global effort, with Randy Lert as the chief investment officer.

The next step was more difficult, as it involved reengineering the company using Andersen Consulting to help us identify our priorities. Obviously, it had never been a secret to us that we could make more money as an asset manager, with a potentially unlimited client base, than we could as a consultant, with a clientele limited to 40 (or later, 50) large pension plans. Everybody knew that in 1980 when we launched Frank Russell Trust Company. However, it was quite another matter for senior management to say explicitly, "Frank Russell Company is an investment manager." We continued to acknowledge our consulting heritage: Manager research was the *heart* of our operation, but investment management was designated our *engine of growth*. And, within investment management, Mike identified what he called "The Vital Two": V1 was institutional investment management sold directly by Russell, and V2 was retail distribution sold indirectly through partners.

With these new priorities in place, the institutional sales force began to focus on larger pension funds with assets of $1 billion and more. And we began to reach out more to endowments and foundations as well as retirement plans.

In the U.S. we began to sign up a new type of distribution partner to reach a broader audience of individual investors than we could via regional banks and registered advisors. At the time, selling

Russell funds through broker-dealers seemed a radical departure. But we took care to pick the right partners—A. G. Edwards and Raymond James, for example—and the alliances have worked well for all concerned.

Mike also decided to initiate a global distribution strategy. Our first partner outside the U.S. was Richardson-Greenshields, a Canadian brokerage firm that was later acquired by Royal Bank of Canada. Under Mike's direction, Frank Russell Company established global funds domiciled in the Cayman Islands and in Dublin, Ireland, enabling us to sell in markets virtually anywhere in the world. Global partners included Société Générale for distribution in Europe. As I said, Mike is a great negotiator, so all of these deals seemed to go smoothly and work out well.

Mike also identified Frank Russell Securities as a key source of ongoing revenue, rather than an ancillary enterprise. To refresh your memory, we entered the brokerage business in 1969 when we began consulting—to give clients a way to pay their consulting fees by directing a portion of their trades through us. Then, in managing our funds, we developed techniques for keeping costs down when changing managers in our own portfolios. This developed into our standalone transition management business, which has been a very successful enterprise for us. By promoting Russell Securities to V3—the third vital element in our business strategy—Mike developed a key source of income that kept the company profitable during the bear market of 2000–2001.

Continuity of Culture

In growing the company, Mike Phillips did a great job of keeping the Russell culture intact. We had a very similar understanding about the central importance of the people in the organization. As Mike puts it,

> There's a feeling at Russell that we're all on the same team and that there is a respect for people. And the balance in people's lives. I think that's the first thing. The second thing is, and George exemplified this and was the role model for

> me: Don't put profit above everything else. Don't put return maximization above everything else. And when in doubt, go for what is right, for society and your customers' interest, not what is right for your interest. Those are the critical things in the culture that I believe exist at Russell.

This is not to say that there weren't significant changes when Mike took over as CEO. By formalizing our research and investment processes, the company became, by definition, less entrepreneurial. But that's exactly what you'd expect from a company that's starting to mature. With the naming of The Vital Two, some of the people who had important roles, but weren't involved in the investment business, definitely read this as bad news for them and their part of the enterprise. In a way, it was similar to the situation we faced when we first launched the Trust Company. I went around to each client individually; I explained that they were still important and I promised that they would benefit from the change. In this case, our challenge was to reassure our associates that all of them remained important. This was objectively true. We couldn't run our funds properly without the intellectual capital we built in our manager research and consulting operations. Most of the people involved in those operations understood and accepted the proposition. A few did not, and they left the company.

Another element of the culture that changed is what Mike would describe as "the family orientation" that Jane and I brought to the company. In the old days, if you were loyal and kept your nose clean and worked hard, that was usually enough. If you weren't all that productive, we'd usually try to find another role that you could handle.

Mike came and talked to me about the need to make Frank Russell Company more meritocratic. In other words, he wanted to fire people who weren't productive. He argued that a business is not a family. In a family, you don't fire your kid. But in a growing, competitive business, we simply couldn't afford to carry everyone as we had before.

Selling the Company

The process of selling Frank Russell Company really began in 1989, at the same executive committee meeting that anointed Mike as my successor. As you'll recall, the executive committee took only about five minutes to choose him. The rest of the discussion focused on the shortcomings of my will in providing a proper succession of ownership in the event of my death. I have four adult children: Sarah, Richard, Eric, and Dion. With the exception of Dion, all of them have had roles in the company at various times. Sarah focused on corporate philanthropy, and directed our initial efforts to set up a family foundation, as you'll see in Chapter 10. Richard played various roles connected to marketing—most critically leading the group that created our mission statement, "Improving financial security for people." Eric is the only one who worked full-time for a period of years in the company. He helped establish our office in Sydney. Then he came back to Tacoma and directed our initiative in the defined contribution segment. Dion has always been focused on education; she founded the Lighthouse Christian School, which educates 325 children of elementary and middle-school age here in Gig Harbor. Ultimately, we agreed that none of our children wanted to devote their lives to running Frank Russell Company.

The executive committee had seen right away that it was a mistake in our wills to leave ownership of the company within my family. If that wasn't enough, we realized that if Jane and I died still owning the company, our successors would be forced to sell it immediately just to pay estate taxes. Thus, we put in place a long-term plan to sell the company.

We hired Goldman Sachs in 1998 and asked them to explore two possibilities: an IPO or a friendly buyout.

As we got more deeply into the process, I began to realize that going public had some significant drawbacks. In a public company, the CEO and the chairman have to spend a significant percentage of their time talking publicly about the company, explaining why it is going in this or that direction. You have to allocate a lot of time just to convince shareholders that they should continue to hold onto their shares.

The other negative part is that publicly traded stocks go up and down. I liked the idea of stability in the economic side of the equation—particularly for our associates: I felt they would be much more comfortable if their ownership was a stable asset and not one that was unpredictable.

About six months into the process, we notified Goldman Sachs that we had decided against an IPO, but that they should continue with their efforts to find a qualified buyer. Here, our criteria were essentially identical to the ones we used for choosing the CEO to replace me. We were looking for an organization with compatible values: non-negotiable integrity, the ability to thrive in a changing environment, a buyer that was global in its thinking, and that treated people fairly and was not overly focused on the bottom line. We weren't looking for an exact dollar figure so much as a merger of similar organizations and an easy transfer of capital so that there would be no interruption in the course and speed of the operation.

Eventually we narrowed the field to four or five candidates. Some of the suitors were large banks with headquarters in other countries. A few of these actually made higher offers than the one we eventually accepted. But there was a cultural fit with Northwestern Mutual that made its offer much more appealing to us than any of the others.

Northwestern Mutual had some of the same cultural history that we did. A mutual life insurance company headquartered in Milwaukee, Wisconsin, they had been in business since 1857— much longer than we had been. Obviously, they were very stable and they filled the role of the largest employer in downtown Milwaukee, just as we did in Tacoma.

From a business perspective, we viewed our core competencies as complementary, not competitive. The related notion was that they would not send anybody from Milwaukee to work at Frank Russell and we wouldn't send anybody from Frank Russell Company to work in Northwestern Mutual. They didn't even want to change our name.

It really was a good fit. But we still had to close the deal.

Closing the Deal—Complementary Skills

We got to the final point in early August 1998. This was when Mike Phillips really showed his worth as a negotiator. We were preparing our final offer, but we were still not happy about a couple of details. Our advisor from Goldman Sachs counseled us that these were important, and we had to make sure they were included in the agreement.

Unknown to us, Jim Ericson, the CEO of Northwestern Mutual, had just met with the trustees, who had authorized him to offer a certain set of terms, but nothing more. Remember, this was happening at the height of the bull market in 1998: The terms were *very* good. But there were limits. The trustees had said that this was enough. They wouldn't go any higher.

Mike and I were on a conference call with Jim Ericson and John Schlifske, who was one of the key people at Northwestern working on the deal. Now remember, I was under orders from Goldman to continue negotiating. So I said, "Jim, it's nice to hear from you. I think we're making a lot of progress. But there are two more things that we want to talk to you about, and I'm going to have Mike Phillips explain those."

I looked over at Mike and it was like one of those cartoons where you can see the wheels turning inside the character's head. A few seconds later, Mike started speaking without any prompting or agreement with me. He said, "Jim, we're very disappointed, obviously, that in these two areas we can't seem to persuade you to give us what we need. But we know that in this type of deal, we have to leave something on the table for goodwill. And so we accept your terms."

I was stunned. I thought Mike must have gone crazy. Then I heard Jim Ericson's response. He said, "I am delighted. And I have to tell you that I disbanded my trustees group this morning and if there had been any further negotiation, I have to tell you that we would not have been willing to go forward."

Mike's skill as a negotiator and his confidence in his intuition turned out to be lucky for us. Within two weeks of signing the definitive agreement, the market cracked. The value of asset management companies declined, and it would have been difficult for us to match the offer we accepted. Northwestern Mutual profited too, as our growth rate continued at its historical rate for many years following the change of ownership.

Did I mention that Northwestern Mutual paid entirely in cash? It was a clean deal for $1 billion.

Moving Forward

It was a novel feeling to be working for someone else. I hadn't experienced that since my grandfather died, 40 years earlier. Under the terms of the deal, I stayed on as chairman of the board. I kept this position until 2002, when Mike assumed the role.

The first board meeting took place not too long after the transaction closed, but I was out of town and had to chair the meeting by phone. Mike attended in person in Milwaukee. The meeting lasted for two hours. At the end of it, I said to Jim, "There's only one difference that I notice between pre-acquisition and post-acquisition."

Jim said, "Well, George, what is that?"

"Well," I said, "this meeting lasted about two hours; in the 40-plus years that I was in charge of board meetings at Frank Russell Company, I don't ever remember a meeting that lasted longer than two minutes."

Of course Northwestern Mutual had formal board meetings where they would listen to detailed reports from the CFO and other division leaders. In our case, being privately owned, we took care of the financials separately, on a regular basis. I would just have our general counsel write up the minutes and bring them up to my office, and I would sign them.

Later, I asked Mike what Jim Ericson's facial expression was when he heard that. Mike just smiled. He understood that long meetings are not my cup of tea—and how much fun it can be to tease your boss.

Obviously, there always was some give-and-take in my relationship with Mike. We accepted that as a result of the autonomy we both demanded. We were able to work together with a high level of mutual respect because, ultimately, we shared a common set of values. Says Mike:

> Part of what I learned from George and part of what I just feel in my core—was respect for people. George was profoundly of the mind that the main interaction between us as people in this company should be based on the respect that we have for each other as human beings. And I would make that specific with an illustration: The CEO makes more than the person running the mailroom, but that's just market pricing. It's not to be confused with the worth of the human being. George always fundamentally understood that, and I did, too.

I'd say we were pretty well aligned when it came to our view of people.

Key Points from Chapter 8

1. *Hire your replacement* is an effective strategy for maintaining continuity at every level and every functional area in your business.
2. Leadership transitions take time. Start planning well in advance in order to give yourself the leeway to backtrack if necessary.
3. Once you've chosen a successor, take the time needed for training and introducing "the new boss" to all stakeholders.
4. A bit of friction is to be expected. If you start hearing jokes at your expense, that's a good sign. Take it with good humor— and dish out some of your own.
5. Keep looking forward. If you've chosen well, the company will do fine without you. And you'll be free to focus your attention on new challenges and interests.

Take Risks

"REAL ENTREPRENEURS NEVER STOP."

When the people of Berlin tore down the Wall in November 1989, there were characteristic reactions around the world. For the most part, everyone celebrated. Francis Fukuyama published a controversial essay, entitled "The End of History," in which he declared that liberal democracy had triumphed over totalitarian Marxism once and for all. Of course, the Marxists—at least the ones who operated from secure perches in places like France and the U.S.—shot back with their own retorts.

But in the countries that were at last free of the burden of a centrally planned command economy, an enormous unleashing of the human spirit, and its attendant entrepreneurial energy, was taking place. The map of Europe changed overnight. Old names reappeared: St. Petersburg, Russia, the Ukraine, and Georgia. And the great capitals of central Europe, such as Warsaw, Budapest, and Prague, regained the luster of autonomy. Last, but not least, the adjectives *East* and *West* disappeared, and Berlin stood reunited.

New Opportunities

That moment was also a pivotal one for Frank Russell Company, and for me, personally, as a leader. Markets were strong, and business was doing well. We had successfully leveraged our core consulting expertise into funds, data, and securities subsidiaries. And we'd established a global presence with offices in London, Toronto, Sydney, and Tokyo. I had handed off day-to-day responsibilities to Mike Phillips; my focus was now more strategic. It would have been easy to be complacent, to take a low-risk approach that sought only to maximize profits in the existing businesses.

As you know by now, that's not my style. And in general, "running in place" is not a strategy that I'd recommend to any business. Markets have a way of moving ahead when you least expect it; trying to maintain a status quo is an almost-certain recipe for being left behind. After all, that's one of the lessons of the Berlin Wall.

At the same time, I never believed in trying to maximize growth at any cost. As I've stated before, I am comfortable making strategic decisions that involve major risks, including the loss of capital, adverse publicity, and missed opportunities. However, I never wanted to take on debt in order to finance new ventures. There were two exceptions, which I've already mentioned. Both occurred early in the company's history: first, when I had to borrow to buy out my father's controlling interest, and later, when we purchased a seat on the New York Stock Exchange. In each case, we retired the debt as quickly as possible.

That's a different philosophy than that of most corporations today. They tend to build up their debt, thinking they can grow faster if they borrow the money to push things along. I never had that feeling. I wanted zero debt because we were in a business that related to the stock market. If you have a lot of debt and then the market happens to go down and your business slows, your operating revenue declines—and then what are you going to do to cover your debt? I decided to eliminate that possibility. I paid back the loan for the NYSE seat in six months and then never took on any debt after that.

I guess you could say that our strategy for growth was organic in the sense that we were always able to expand using existing resources. For example, once we had figured out how to research

U.S. equity managers, it wasn't that big a leap to expand our capability to international managers and open up a new asset class for our clients.

After we had established a successful consulting practice for U.S. pension funds, we didn't have to stretch too far to set up something similar in the UK. We kept costs down by requiring Jan Twardowski to live and work in the same apartment in the outskirts of London. So we were taking a business risk, but using an incremental approach to manage our financial exposure.

We faced much bigger challenges when branching out to the investment management business, because of the legal expenses and the cost of building infrastructure. However, the key part of fund management—the intellectual capital—was already in place. That meant the biggest risk was the possibility of alienating our consulting clients, which we managed by staking our personal integrity on the promise that they would always remain a focal point for us.

With this type of organic growth, you risk capital and reputation. But the consequences of failure are largely limited to the new venture. If you are not burdened with debt, if the corporate culture is intact and the firm's integrity is not questioned, then the enterprise can sustain quite a bit of entrepreneurial risk-taking. In fact, the enterprise may *require* a periodic infusion of risk to keep its competitive edge.

The Inspiration of John Mroz

In those heady days as communism breathed its final gasp, I attended a conference in Sun Valley. It was in the spring of 1990, and John Mroz was the guest speaker. John is a peacemaker who, in my opinion, deserves the Nobel Prize: What he has accomplished is mind-boggling. He founded the EastWest Institute in 1980 and, at the time of the conference, had been meeting with Viktor Yushchenko, the new president of Ukraine, advising him on how to build and maintain ties with Russia. John has worked to bring the Palestinians and Israelis together. And after

9/11, I joined a group that John organized, including former U.S. Senators Boren, Simpson, and Danforth, which talked to President Putin and his defense minister, Ivanov, and then met with President Bush. This effort helped to build a bridge for high-level communication between Russia and the United States.

Some of Mr. Putin's recent stances are disappointing to those of us who had hoped for and worked to bring about a permanent thaw in East-West relations. But John harbored no illusions. His talk in Sun Valley focused on the chaotic situation behind the Iron Curtain. He spoke of things the CIA didn't know about. John Kenneth Galbraith at Harvard had just published a book saying the Soviet economy was stronger than ours; John Mroz avoided that mistake. Just look at the EastWest Institute's mission statement: "We work to make the world a safer place by addressing the seemingly intractable problems that threaten regional and global stability." Those words betray a pragmatic sensibility that understands that history has not ended. The task of bringing people together is one that's likely to be with us for quite some time.

Listening to John in Sun Valley made me reflect on how opening new markets and transacting business helps to forge relationships among people with otherwise different interests and ways of looking at the world. I was so excited and impressed that I woke up at 2 A.M. with the idea for a new venture fully developed in my head—literally everything, including the name: "Russell 20-20."

The Opportunity of a Lifetime

The concept was pretty simple. Nearly three billion people lived in countries emerging from command economies, including Russia, the former Soviet satellite nations in Central Europe, India (which was closely connected with Russia at that time), and China. The opening of these markets had a potential economic impact more or less comparable to the discovery of the New World five centuries earlier. Along with the industrial and technological revolutions, it represented one of the greatest business opportunities in history.

I saw this clearly. I also knew from my experience with institutional investors that almost all of them have a problem finding the time needed to visit new business opportunities in person to "kick the tires." My idea was to take a trip once a year to do onsite research. We'd call ourselves Russell 20-20, because our group would consist of 20 corporate pension funds and 20 money managers. Because of the size of the assets we represented, we would command a certain level of attention from government leaders and business interests. That way, we could get the access we needed to learn firsthand about the investment opportunities in those countries. We wanted to meet the leaders and see factories. It was an attempt to educate ourselves, to advance the learning process.

It took me 41 phone calls to secure our 40 members. Everyone was eager to jump right in. The asset managers were concerned with how and when to invest; the corporate members might have an interest in doing business in these countries.

I brought in Joan Sobba to manage the organizational side and hired a retired general, Joe Ulatoski, as co-director; he was the scout and logistics person out in the field. In 1992, we took our first trip to Prague and Warsaw. Members who participated in that first trip remember the circumstances vividly. "The Russian troops were actually physically leaving Prague as we arrived there," recalls Russell 20-20 member emeritus Stephen Braswell, who, at the time of that first visit, represented Prudential Investment Management. "On the site visits in Prague, we were basically going in and looking at many of the state-run industries. They were in shambles. They had lost virtually all of their market, and were almost deserted."

Another dramatic revelation for participants was the lack of exposure, throughout these economies, to the language and practice of capitalism: Business plans, along with knowledge of competitive pressures and consumer demands for products, were nowhere in sight. Gaps in understanding were demonstrated by many of the businesses visited. In Poland, the delegation broke into smaller groups to visit various sites in and around Warsaw. Russell 20-20 executive committee member Vera Trojan, who headed emerging markets investments for Wellington Management Company, was also on that first trip.

Vera's group visited a factory that made coats to order for German designers. The owner of this operation showed them around personally. The work floor was clean and well organized, and he had a health clinic set up for his workers. For Vera, this was a man who was proud of how well his business was running, and who took a paternal interest in his workers. He invited the group to lunch—bringing them upstairs to his personal offices, where the table was set with decorations of Polish and American flags. "We were all feeling very positive," Vera recounts, "and as we sat down at the lunch, he said, 'Welcome to everybody, and *could you please tell me why you're all here?*'"

Access Matters

The countries Russell 20-20 visited early on soon learned about investments and investors. A good example is the group's visit to South Africa in 2003. Brian Davis, who took over the director role in 2000, was building the itinerary for that trip. The gatekeeper for the South African government urged Brian to schedule *four hours* with South African President Thabo Mbeki. "He offered the group an entire half-day with the president," Brian recalls. "I replied to him, 'I can't imagine he's not busy—how about one hour?' We settled on two—and the session went very well."

Over the years, Russell 20-20 has met with scores of heads of state and cabinet ministers: from President Mbeki to former Prime Minister Mahathir bin Mohamad of Malaysia, to former Russian Prime Ministers Mikhail Kasyanov and Sergei Kiriyenko, to now-retired Chinese Premier Zhu Rongji, the architect of the China-opening campaign. Each meeting, regardless of the literal content communicated, provided useful macro information.

Members also gleaned specific information that was extremely valuable in shaping their investment opinions. Ralph Layman, who was executive vice president, international equities at GE Asset Management, recalls an exceptional exchange during the 20-20 visit to Malaysia in 2000. The group met with Mahathir bin Mohamad, Malaysia's highly controversial prime minister. During the Q&A session, Mahathir tried to evade—but finally answered—a question Ralph posed. "Essentially, he responded that he didn't care about capital markets—he only wanted foreign direct investment into Malaysia. This was exactly what I thought, but for him to be that blunt and say it directly—at the time, it was impactful," Ralph says.

Vera Trojan recalls another edifying exchange. The group visited Russia for the second time in May 1998, just when the entire political and financial system was unraveling. Prime Minister Sergei Kiriyenko had just been appointed by President Yeltsin; he would ultimately hold this role for less than six months.

Russell 20-20's meeting with Kiriyenko was an eye-opener. "Just seeing him and watching him struggle with these issues was very helpful in understanding what was at stake—and what means the government had to deal with this," says Vera. "This was a critical point for Russia; we were there as it was rolling into crisis. Visiting a country at that kind of a turning point, and being able to talk to peers who are trying to figure this out as well, and seeing the leadership struggle with the same thing—this was very useful for us."

But as any Russell 20-20 member will confirm, hearing from heads-of-state and cabinet ministers can never provide the whole picture. Balanced access also includes hearing from people who are doing business on the ground in these countries. W. Allen Reed, who was president and CEO of General Motors Asset Management, describes a case in point. Russell 20-20 participants were attending a dinner on the 2003 South Africa trip. During the course of the dinner, a government speaker painted a fairly rosy picture of the country's struggles in its transition from apartheid.

"The CEO of a local South African–based business was sitting next to me at dinner, and he shared with me the somewhat different perspective that he had," recalls Allen. "When you can get down to the level of a one-on-one with someone who's talking to you in a non-public situation, you often get a different story. If you ask the right questions, you can get more out of these trips than the 'official' message. At times, that has been the most valuable piece of information that I've received."

In some cases, it's simply the ability to observe first hand. GE's Ralph Layman recalls a series of site visits in Chongqing to local companies that were the product of joint ventures with multinational companies. "Briggs & Stratton was one that really stuck out as an interesting joint venture," says Ralph. "It had struggled at the beginning, and the Chinese management that took it over localized it. Yet we could see that they had the same values that a Briggs & Stratton plant in the U.S. would have: fundamentals like management incentives, safety, quality, profitability."

Ralph continues,

> The slogans that were all over the campus for this fractional horsepower engine factory were very similar to what you might have seen at GE back in the United States. In the center of China, here were many of the same values that we were looking for in our company. The locals were running it. And it was profitable—in fact, they were doing extremely well. That, to me, was an indication that the tide was turning. The old song about China—that you can go there and set up shop but you'll never make money—was beginning to be debunked from a bottom-up basis.

It's hard to remember that, throughout the 1990s, people were wondering if their investments in China would ever pay off. Clearly, Russell 20-20 enabled its members to get into these markets early—a wise decision from today's perspective, one decade later.

Russell's Venture in Alternative Investing

While I'm still a proponent of investing in emerging markets, they truly require an experienced team with the ability to manage the different types of risk involved. Russell 20-20 first visited

China in May 1993. At about the same time we became partners in a private equity venture called the Asian Infrastructure Fund. To support our efforts, we formed a new business unit called Russell Capital, which eventually included all of our alternative investment activities such as hedge funds and real estate private partnerships.

We selected a three-person team to direct this new venture. Hal Strong had recently joined Russell, bringing strong investment banking experience from Piper, Jaffrey, Hopwood and Salomon Brothers. Paul Kaltinick, as usual, was our go-to guy when it came to launching new businesses. Don Hardy rounded out the team, providing leadership in research and development. Don had been with us since 1977, as one of our first researchers of fixed-income managers. He later followed Jan Twardowski to London, where he directed our European operations for five years in the mid-1980s. As part of that assignment, he had worked on a consulting project for one of Australia's most-respected companies, Lend Lease. The results were so successful that Lend Lease became a major relationship for us—a fact that led directly to our establishing a new office in Sydney in 1986.

When Don returned to Tacoma, he took the reins of another new business, Russell Private Investments (RPI), which focused on developing investment strategies for individuals, families, and foundations. Hedge funds were part of RPI's mandate, so one of Don's responsibilities was to apply Russell's research methodology to the often-arcane world of hedge fund managers. Alternative assets present a unique challenge because they do not lend themselves to quantitative analysis. Private equity is particularly difficult because the assets are not priced on a regular basis. Without a record of price movements, you can't measure volatility in a meaningful way. Don Ezra explained this humorously at one of Russell Capital's Private Equity Seminars. Using the analogy of "eating well" for high investment returns and "sleeping well" for effective risk management, Don observed that private equity is "an illiquid market that occasionally suddenly changes," when the manager sells a position. As such, investors are "in a deep sleep, but they are sleeping well artificially, as if they'd been given sleeping pills." The information comes only later when the investor "wakes up" to the news of the investment outcomes. "You can calculate information ratios from whatever parameters you measure, but they're not reliable because the body is asleep for the most part."

To put it directly: Our tools for measuring risk were not effective in these alternative asset classes.

On the one hand, that's what made entering this business so risky for us. We couldn't easily adapt many of our existing methods to this new asset class. In managing alternatives, would we be able to maintain the high standards that our clients had come to expect? On the other hand, alternatives were a tremendous opportunity precisely because they involved greater risks. Throughout our history we had always been able to develop tools that allowed investors to pioneer new markets and asset classes, while managing the risk prudently, with insight and discipline. There was simply no way we could back away from the challenge.

Asset Allocation *is* Rocket Science

One of the key breakthroughs in risk management came from a wholly unexpected source. Peter Dietz called from our then-fledgling office in Tokyo with an unusual problem. A Japanese insurance company was trying to manage their assets and get control over their earnings statement and balance sheet. Their problem had become so serious that they feared it might become a regulatory matter, which in turn could cause them to lose market share.

The person Peter called was Andy Turner, who had joined Russell about five years earlier, in 1984. In his previous role as a tenured professor, Andy had focused on corporate finance and derivative securities. However, Peter knew that Andy was interested in pursuing practical applications, so he gave him a call and put him to work counseling our clients who were interested in "synthetic cash" and portfolio insurance strategies. Andy also analyzed the pros and cons of incentive fees and produced valuable research on tactical asset allocation.

Much of this work is complicated mathematically—certainly well beyond my capacity—and it was important that we could be a reliable guide to our clients in these areas. That's why we made Andy our Director of Research in 1988.

Now the problem for Yasuda Fire and Marine was that conventional asset allocation, using the Markowitz paradigm of risk, wasn't working for them. This has always been a basic shortcoming in the Markowitz model. If variance is your measure of risk, it implies that clients are bothered equally by surprises to both the upside and the downside. Obviously, that's not the case. People love excess returns and hate losing money, so clearly the risk is not symmetrical.

Also, in the real world, financial events happen at odd intervals. People save for any number of things like college tuition, remodeling a house, or a well-deserved vacation. All the while, retirement lurks in the background. With traditional asset-allocation models, you're forced to choose one event—usually retirement—and ignore the others.

This was a daunting challenge, and at the time no one had made much progress toward solving it for an individual investor or a relatively straightforward pension fund, let alone a complex situation like Yasuda presented. So, when Peter told Mr. Sasimoto, "Yes, there's another way of solving the problem," he was acting in the great Russell tradition of accepting a major risk without knowing precisely how he was going to find the solution. As Andy recounts,

> At the time I did have an idea, although what we actually ended up doing was technically quite a bit different from my original idea. I went back to material I had learned in graduate school and then forward in the literature with the help of a couple of researchers. We ended up adapting techniques that were well proven in other areas such as rocket science and targeting.

In fact, Andy had recently hired a brilliant young man named David Carino, whose background was in the defense industry and who had a Ph.D. in operations research from Stanford. David was very familiar with the ideas and the techniques that we needed. For example, we had to create a system of approximately 110,000 equations that described how their business worked—how money moved through time and through different accounts within Yasuda.

The task was so huge that we also brought in people from IBM and from a couple of universities. But in the end we cracked the code. Our new style of optimization program—multiperiod stochastic optimization—was the first to allow clients to incorporate realistic scenarios into their asset allocation scenario. The Yasuda Model allows you to input multiple goals, tempered by a realistic assessment of how the client feels about those goals, with the level of importance changing at different points in time. Yasuda loved it and it also won a prestigious Franz Edelman award in 1993.

The Final Frontier?

Sophisticated tools such as the Yasuda Model can help investors understand and manage risk—but not eliminate it. Diversification, too, has its limits. In the early days of Russell 20–20, I used to give a speech where I said words to the effect that *the opening of these markets will be the greatest investment opportunity until young people find a way to live and work off the planet.* I still believe that. However, not long after, one of the financial journals ran a satirical article on the use of "extraterrestrial equities" to mitigate portfolio risk. They fabricated an efficient frontier diagram, similar to the ones we use. And they cited me in a footnote!

I take their point. Diversification is an effective tool for smoothing your return pattern. But ultimately you have to be in the market. If the market goes down, you will have losses. We never told our clients otherwise.

Of course, the risks increase when investments are exotic and basic information is not available. Andy Turner noted this at the Russell Capital Seminar at Harvard in 1998. He cautioned that statistical models for private equity were unreliable due to the limited data on benchmarks and expected returns. And he talked about the potential of multistage stochastic programming with recourse—the Yasuda Model—to help private equity investors make meaningful asset-allocation decisions.

This effort was only partially successful. As Don Ezra noted, "It gives you a richer model, but you're still stuck with the same basic uncertainty about what your inputs are." Over time, Don and his colleague, John Ilkiw, evolved a solution they called "Two-Stage Asset Allocation." In Stage I, where reliable market data is available, investors use tools like the Yasuda Model to decide broad market asset class exposures. Then, in Stage II, investors can choose to replace part of their equity allocation with private equity, if they believe the exposure will enhance their returns. Russell's default recommendation was to place 10 percent of the client's equities in alternatives.

Significantly, John Ilkiw observed, "what really drives [private equity] returns is the success of active management." This pretty much mirrors my own view, that the keys to success in alternatives are avoiding overconfidence and performing diligent qualitative research on investment managers.

We've recently seen examples of complex strategies, managed by brilliant, sophisticated investors—that have failed spectacularly. After the fact, we learn that these products had been stress-tested and performed well in something like 99.9 percent of historical scenarios. That 0.1 percent scenario is triggered only if something outlandish happens, such as a major government defaulting on its sovereign debt. Or it could have been something else—a war, a natural disaster, a worldwide banking collapse. These "unlikely" scenarios are sometimes called *fat-tail events* because they occur out on the extreme edges of a return distribution; instead of a traditional bell curve, where the tails dwindle away to almost nothing, some investment strategies have fat tails that represent a sharp increase in the risk level.

Over time, even a relatively risky investment strategy can prevail, as long as it's not excessively leveraged. The fat-tail scenario will not permanently damage a portfolio that's not overly encumbered with debt. But it will be fatal to a portfolio that's leveraged 200:1, or even 50:1. So avoid overconfidence.

My other admonition has to do with careful manager selection. When Don Hardy first began researching hedge funds, he came upon a product that had been widely recommended to Russell clients by a previous consultant. The hedge fund in question had a fabulous track record: 11 to 12 percent per year with almost no volatility of return. It was too good to be true, and that made Don suspicious:

> I had developed a couple of rules for evaluating hedge funds. Number one, the hedge fund manager/general partner should have a significant part of his liquid net worth in the fund on a side-by-side basis with his investors. And number two, every product should have an audit by a recognized firm specializing in hedge funds.

In this case, the fund didn't meet either of those criteria. In spite of the strong returns, Don recommended terminating the fund in all of our client accounts. The wisdom of this decision became apparent 15 months later:

> I picked up the *Wall Street Journal* on Monday morning and saw a story about this fund. It had imploded. The manager claimed to follow a fairly conservative strategy of buying and selling options against fixed income instruments. Instead, he'd gone wild and was buying naked options on extremely volatile stocks, and lost all his money. It was a $300 million fund and it went to zero almost overnight.

I take particular encouragement from this story. In constructing our research operation, I always felt that at least 60 percent of the useful information we collected came from the qualitative side of our process. A fraudulent manager will, most likely, know how to fake all of the numbers. You may be able to pick up some clues, but, as in this example, it will be the qualitative discipline that really protects you. No audit? No commitment of their own money? Move along to another opportunity.

With discipline and prudence, the long-term investment story remains a compelling one. The same is true of the prospects for entrepreneurs and businesspeople in general. Rewards continue to be available to those willing to take reasonable calculated risks.

All of this is captured neatly in an anecdote that Andy Turner recounted to me recently. He reminded me of the banquet that our friends at Yasuda held for us at the conclusion of the project. Everybody was lined up by rank. I sat with Jane on one side and Andy on the other.

A server came out and announced that the chef had prepared a seasonal delicacy. There were two enormous tureens with something swimming in them, possibly baby eels or very small fish. In front of us they placed individual cups with a small tab extending from the lip so you could pick it up. These cups were filled with a pink viscous liquid that smelled a bit pungent, like hot-and-sour soup.

The first to be served was Mr. Sasimoto, who was sitting across from Andy. The server took a dip net and scooped up a helping of these live animals from the tureen and dropped them into Sasimoto's cup. The minute they hit this liquid there was a violent thrashing with bubbles steaming to the surface. Sasimoto picked up his cup and slurped it down.

Andy was next. I wasn't quite sure how he'd handle it, so I watched closely.

Andy turned to our host and said with exquisite politeness, "Mr. Sasimoto, please teach me."

Sasimoto looked at Andy with a serious expression and said, "Swallow, don't chew."

You could see Andy repeating that to himself like a mantra, "Swallow, don't chew. Swallow, don't chew." They filled his cup and he slurped it right down, just as he had been instructed.

Now he looked at me: I appeared to be dismayed and struggling to conceal my resentment that he had not come up with some excuse—allergies or fatigue or something—that would have allowed us both to have weaseled out of that soup without losing face. That's Andy's take.

Looking back, I can't rule out the possibility that thoughts like that might have crossed my mind. I simply don't remember. What I know for sure is this: Recalling the odd sensation of those slippery little fish or eels squirming their way down, makes me think that there are still significant differences between cultures—even those with formal business ties and similar political ideologies. History is not dead; it never will die. Diversification remains valid, with or without extraterrestrial equities, and there will always be plenty of work for John Mroz and others like him—the peacemakers—whose mission is to build bridges between nations.

Key Points from Chapter 9

1. Continue to take risks. If you try to maintain the status quo, your competitors will do their best to make you obsolete, irrelevant, and unprofitable.
2. Avoid excessive debt: It can be a fatal burden during periods when your core business is slow.
3. When possible, leverage existing capabilities into new areas. For example, you can introduce your core product into new markets, or adapt it for different segments of users.
4. In researching risks and opportunities, there's no substitute for in-person inspections and face-to-face meetings.

CHAPTER 10

Have Fun

"THE IDEAL OF A BALANCED LIFE."

first described these 10 elements of success to an audience of investment advisors. It was November 1996, and Frank Russell Company was just launching its first-ever national advertising campaign with a two-page spread in the *Wall Street Journal.* When I reached item number 10, "Have Fun," I said, "I assume you have fun in your non-business life; why not double that fun at business?" And I showed them the central image from our new ad: three climbers roped together on the icy edge of a mountain. The summit is up there, always the goal, but on this particular picture there is a vertical fall on the left and a steep fall in the right.

I said, "I will tell you what you want: You want to know each of those climbers. You want them to be knowledgeable in mountain climbing, trained and experienced. It's a team working together. You share total mutual trust. Your life is at stake. There is no question about it. You have to trust your teammates. That's the way it should be in your business."

I further explained that, with Mike Phillips as my key teammate leading Russell, "I can have fun out on the edge of the envelope." Because that sense of freedom was, for me, so powerful and professionally invigorating, I wanted to share it with all of our associates.

Fun in the Himalayas

The Russell sabbatical program was just over a year old at that time. We had announced the benefit in 1995, but the roots of the idea go back a decade earlier. In early 1985, Jane and I decided to take some time away from the company for our own personal enjoyment. We had been working hard without any extended breaks for a period of several decades. We wanted to refresh ourselves, have fun, and renew our minds and spirits. So we asked Bob Bates and his wife, Gail, to join us on a trip to the Himalayas in February and March of that year—60 glorious days. Bob was familiar with the region from his many climbing expeditions beginning in the 1930s, and he was able to arrange what for me was the experience of a lifetime.

The itinerary included familiar destinations such as the Taj Mahal. As an old India hand, Bob chose to show it to us first from the Agra Fort, because that was where its creator had been exiled. As Bob explained to us, Shah Jehan, the great Mughal ruler, had been deposed by his son; under house arrest, he sat behind the Fort's exquisite marble screens, looking at the Taj Mahal from across the Jumna River—unable to visit it. Thanks to Bob, we were seeing it from this unique historical perspective.

Next, we flew to Kathmandu, where Bob introduced us to the world's most famous mountain climber, Sir Edmund Hillary. Hard to top that, but the following day we visited a wildlife preserve called Tiger Tops, where you fly in and then ride on an elephant's back to your accommodations. The local population included Asian rhinos, a sloth bear, and later in the evening, a tiger "tearing chunks of meat from a kill."

There were physical challenges, highlighted by a three-day trek crossing an 11,000-foot pass. And spiritual exercises, too. In a temple in Bhutan, I imitated the local custom of taking an enormous metal chain on your back: Each link weighed around 50 pounds, and then you'd kneel down and pray, surrounded by wall paintings of, in Bob's words, "demons with eyes on stalks and long necks ending in evil, grinning faces." We also visited a holy site in the Tang Valley, where you can lose all your sins by squeezing through a narrow crevice in the rocks. *We squeezed.*

In Darjeeling, we had the honor of meeting Tenzing Norgay, the Sherpa who accompanied Sir Edmund Hillary on the first ascent of Everest. And the trip concluded with several days of relaxation on a houseboat on Dal Lake, near Srinagar.

The adventure quotient on this trip was off the charts. But for me, the high point was really the opportunity to spend time with my lifelong friend and mentor. Every day was a nonstop conversation with Bob. I don't remember any specific subjects; that wasn't the point. We talked about *everything*—important or trivial, it didn't matter. The moment I treasure most is already described in Bob's book, *The Love of Mountains Is Best*[1], more vividly than I could ever express it:

> On a cold, cloudy morning, George and I were up early to climb Poon Hill to see the sunrise touch the highest points of Dhaulagiri, Annapurna, Nilgiri, and the whole Annapurna Range. It was like watching a tableau. Then, in what was almost a spiritual experience, the rich sunrise glow touched to life one summit and ridge after another, until the whole world seemed a land of hope and promise.

The Russell Sabbatical Program

Back in Tacoma, Jane had one of her characteristic insights. Since our time off had done us so much good, refreshing us spiritually and renewing our enthusiasm about the business, wouldn't it make sense to make sure that our associates had the opportunity to have a similar experience? Of course I had to agree. But what about the costs? There would be an increase in compensation expense of almost two percent across the board, plus we expected that 10 to 15 percent of our people would not return after their time off.

In fact, that attrition rate never materialized. But we knew there was no escaping the logistical problem of losing the services of key people for weeks at a time.

It took nearly 10 years to resolve those issues. But in June 1995, Jane and I were finally able to announce a new benefit for all Russell associates: For every 10 years of service, they earned a two-month sabbatical with no strings attached!

The ways people chose to use their free time were as varied as you might expect. A lot of people traveled. These included car trips in the United States, as well as more far-flung corners of the globe. Several people took trips to the Himalayas. I won't say they were following the example of Jane and me, but I was definitely pleased when I heard about it. One associate even climbed Everest, as far as base camp, which must have been spectacular. I would have loved to have been invited along on that one. A surprising number of people went riding around Ireland on draft horses, and then hopped over to Scotland to see if they could catch a glimpse of the Loch Ness monster.

Other associates stayed closer to home. Some devoted the time to caring for loved ones with serious illnesses. One woman extended her maternity leave to get extra time with her new baby. Others simply relaxed at home.

Several people spent their sabbaticals developing their skills. One associate hit the slopes and got in as much expert ski instruction as he could. Another person studied ceramics in Kyoto, benefiting from a rare opportunity to work directly with master craftsmen who have been designated as Japan's "living national treasures."

Other interesting sabbatical activities included starting a middle school for girls, participating in an archeological dig for dinosaur fossils, and building a British racing car and driving it competitively.

Regardless of the activity—or the lack thereof—the key was providing our associates with the opportunity to have focused, personal time without financial penalty. It was a deliberate effort to promote the ideal of living a balanced life. By encouraging people to have fun, we believed we would be enabling them to improve the quality of their work.

Fun at Work

Meanwhile, back at the office, our work ethic required associates to always strive to exceed client expectations. That's hard work, plain and simple. You have to stay motivated—every day. Benefits like the sabbatical, or even your normal vacation time, are great. But if your clients are beating you over the head with a stick every day, the fact that there are carrots waiting in the distant future may not be enough. You simply have to have fun at work.

Duncan Smith reminded me of an assignment we had accepted in the late 1980s with one of the large public pension funds. As you probably know, our state governments have a formidable number of employees and retirees, and the assets to fund their pension benefits are substantial. In larger states especially, the public funds dwarf their corporate cousins. In theory, this made them ideal clients for us; however, in practice, the governance of public funds is subject to the vagaries of electoral politics, which make it difficult to implement a long-term strategy.

By the second or third meeting, Duncan and I found ourselves feeling frustrated and out of our element in our relationship with our prestigious new public pension fund client. In fact, I remember getting so fed up with the politics around their conference table that I leaned over to Duncan and said, "Let's get out of here."

He said, "I agree."

So I stood up and said, "I'm awfully sorry, but we're resigning from this relationship." And that was the end of it. Duncan later told me that a consultant at one of our competitors thought we were crazy. He said that if his bosses found out he was giving up a quarter-of-a-million-dollar annual fee, he'd get his throat slit.

But I believe that in order to properly serve clients over a long-term relationship, you have to have fun doing it. We were not having fun with the people at this big public fund. Frankly, it was a pain in the—neck. And if I wasn't willing to deal with them, I certainly wasn't willing to ask our associates to accept that kind of continual struggle and pressure. There were plenty of other organizations that we found congenial—corporate funds, endowments, and foundations—as well as banks, advisors, and brokerages serving individual investors, so we didn't suffer too greatly from our decision to avoid this client and the public arena in general. In fact, I'm certain we improved our productivity by eliminating unnecessary stress.

So that was a negative we turned into a positive by walking away. However, there were also aspects of work that I particularly enjoyed—for their own sake.

First of all, I really liked working with Dick Lothrop. As I've already mentioned, Dick was the ultimate peddler. He taught me how to sell. I had the most fun selling a new idea to people who hadn't thought of it—persuading them to accept our approach to solving a problem. Whether it was getting those first 40 clients, or convincing people to set up the Trust Company or to join Russell 20–20, selling was a big part of building our business; it was probably my most enjoyable activity and probably always will be.

The ideas themselves were exciting, too. When we'd come up with something new—whether it was the Dietz Method or private equity investments in Chinese infrastructure—that always gave me a shot of energy. It started with the idea itself, then the development and initial implementation, through the time when it was necessary to hire people smarter than I am to continue the work.

When you think about it, it all comes down to people. Dealing with all of the interesting personalities you encounter in our industry was also quite a bit of fun—at least in retrospect.

For example, our initial insight in 1969 was that it was necessary to establish objective criteria for hiring managers. Sounds pretty simple, right? But then you have to apply that to somebody like Carl Hathaway, who was the superstar equity manager from Morgan Guaranty when we began our consulting practice. Carl was rail-thin, elegantly dressed, keenly intelligent, and impressive in every way. Our analysts recall the impression of merely stepping into his office, which was adorned with exotic items from around the world, such as pachinko machines and elephant tusks.

Carl was widely recognized as the originator of the "nifty-fifty" approach that was producing sizzling returns. As a result, Carl had a supremely self-confident air about him. Paul Kaltinick remembers Carl telling the board at JCPenney that part of his stock-picking technique involved a personal evaluation of the head of every company: If the CEO was overweight, he wouldn't buy the stock!

It was fun taking our new manager evaluation methodology and applying it to someone like Carl Hathaway. You had to strip away the Morgan mystique, the exotic props, the haberdashery, and the bombast and focus instead on the portfolio and the process. I can't remember whether we counseled Paul to fire Morgan in time to avoid the implosion of the nifty-fifty in 1973; but we certainly advised JCPenney to diversify their exposure to a manager who owned a small number of stocks based partly on the percentage of body fat of the CEO!

It was also fun to work closely with true industry innovators like Gordon Binns, the head of General Motors' $50 billion pension fund. Gordon had an academic interest in the theoretical aspects of investments and finance. But he was also an innovator who was open to new strategies and asset classes, and he wasn't afraid to act decisively to implement his ideas. We had a warm, collegial relationship with Gordon and his staff. But imagine what you would have done if you'd been in Mike Phillips' shoes in this unusual scenario. Says Mike:

> Gordon was a traveler. He traveled extensively, around the globe, because he supervised all of GM's pension investments worldwide. I was in Gordon's office one time when he had just come back from Japan. He had a big chair and I was sitting humbly across from him, giving a presentation. Gordon fell asleep with just the two of us in the room. I was faced with this dilemma: One of our most important clients—and a

giant in our industry—had fallen asleep. I couldn't wake him up. That would have been totally inappropriate. I decided the only course of action was to continue, and I completed my presentation with Gordon fast asleep.

As I said, sharing new ideas with clients was one of my favorite parts of the job. And if they showed enough confidence in us to sleep through our quarterly presentation, so much the better!

In addition to selling innovative ideas to exceptionally interesting people, I'd say that bringing Jane into the company was another facet of work that I particularly enjoyed. Jane had a high level of skills in areas where I am deficient. She had such a beautiful and totally natural way of dealing with people: It was fun watching her work. I learned a lot from her. She improved my ability to listen, and helped me realize that people are the most important element of our whole operation. Of course, being able to talk about what happened during the day as we drove home made work far more enjoyable than it would have been without her.

Transition to Philanthropy

Philanthropy is another important way for businesspeople to create balance in their lives. I always enjoyed it when the company made money; I think I enjoyed it even more when we gave money to great causes. And the combination of the two is perfection. I don't know if *fun* is the right word to describe it. *Pleasurable? Rewarding?* As William Blake once wrote in a letter to a friend,

> Fun I love, but . . . mirth is better than fun, and happiness is better than mirth.

At Frank Russell Company, we were *happy* to support a variety of causes, and encouraged associates to get involved on a personal level. The United Way and Habitat for Humanity enjoyed broad support, along with two local art institutions, the Tacoma Art Museum and the Museum of Glass. We encouraged associates to help children in the local schools by authorizing up to one hour off of work each week dedicated to tutoring.

As soon as Mike Phillips came into his own as CEO, I started getting more interested in nonprofit, humanitarian activities, and Jane was enthusiastic about this new direction as well. We established The Russell Family Foundation in anticipation of the day when we would fund it with proceeds from the sale of the company. In the meanwhile, our daughter Sarah took charge of researching similar organizations so that we would be prepared when the time came. We also established an investment entity, called Threshold Group, to manage the assets. Of course, we operate Threshold Group according to our ten essential principles, and I'm pleased to report that we've won numerous awards including Washington CEO's Best Companies To Work For (2004-2008); Seattle Business Magazines'#1 Best Company to Work For in 2009; and recognition as the High Net Worth Advisory/Multi-Family Office of the Year.

Currently, the foundation has three programs for grant making. The first one is named after Jane, and it focuses on the local community—the City of Tacoma and Pierce County. Jane's Fund supports grassroots leadership and many of her longtime favorite community causes. Number two is an environmental sustainability initiative that supports education and green business practices in the Puget Sound region of Washington State. The third fund bears my name and it works globally on peace and security issues, with a particular interest in the countries of Eastern Europe, the former Soviet Union, and Asia Pacific.

In 2008, The Russell Family Foundation made more than $9.7 million in grants in these three areas. These grants will continue in what I hope will be increasing amounts—in perpetuity.

New Adventures: Russian Puppets and Nuclear Waste

I still have a business card. I was never one to sit around and twiddle my thumbs. I don't like to be bored. The back of my card lists a half-dozen organizations where I serve as chairman of the board and three others where I continue in an *emeritus* role.

Bottom line, I'm still having fun. I think I'm involved with some good things, which I'd like to tell you about in the remaining pages of this narrative.

I had been interested in Eastern Europe in general, and Russia in particular, since 1989 and the founding of Russell 20–20. At about that time, I was on the executive committee of the Hoover Institution. In talking with a senior Russian fellow, I asked if anybody was promoting market economics on Russian television. He said, "No," and I replied, "Then we are going to Moscow next week."

I took him to Moscow and we met Basil Grigoriev, who had done an award-winning documentary on Chernobyl. Now he wanted to do a Muppets-type show on Russian television—a funny, engaging way to talk about market economics. I told Basil to go ahead, that I would fund it. Within a few months, *Kukly* was ready to air. It was only 20 minutes per show and only once a week, but it got everybody's attention and, much to everyone's surprise, it became the most popular show on Russian television.

At the same time, Basil wanted to do two documentaries to follow up on his Chernobyl film: one on the Murmansk submarine base and one in Krasnoyarsk, on the Yenisey River in central Russia, where they produce plutonium. These films are startling because they show nuclear waste being treated in the most casual fashion. For example, the clip in Krasnoyarsk shows a couple of nurses delivering babies; then one of them opens up the curtains and there are some boxes outside—a big line of boxes full of nuclear waste.

That sparked an idea. I became obsessed with the need to destroy nuclear waste. Of course, the scientific consensus was that it couldn't be destroyed; it would have to be buried. But I started asking some physicists: Why is that? What keeps us from trying to find out how to destroy it? At the time, people in the United States were trying to agree on a disposal site. But nobody wanted it in their backyard, so nothing was getting done. And nobody could give a satisfactory answer to why there was not an effort to destroy nuclear waste.

It took a long time, but John Mroz finally set up a meeting in 1999 in Dubnu, Russia, which is a nuclear center. We brought together 10 top nuclear scientists for a day and a half to try to answer the question: Can nuclear waste be destroyed? This time, I didn't have to pretend that I wouldn't give them the restroom key until they solved the problem. They did it on their own. At the end of the day and a half, they said, "We think in a decade that could happen."

Back in the U.S., I found transmutation technologists and hired a professor of nuclear science at the University of North Carolina to run a new company called Nuclear Fuel Cycle Technologies. I have been funding that for five years. Right now, we may be less than a year away from testing the theory. If it does work, we'll have a much less serious problem for power in the world, because nuclear is the cheapest, most efficient way to create power. In addition, there are two billion people, out of six billion people on the planet, who don't have fresh water. With safe nuclear power, you could build small nuclear plants on the rivers of Africa and use reverse osmosis to have fresh water available for everyone.

EastWest Institute

Over the years, John Mroz and I became ever more closely connected. He was a frequent speaker at Russell 20–20 events, and I always paid attention to his efforts with the EastWest Institute (EWI). In 1999, John asked me to join the board of EWI; my first board meeting was on May 24 that year. I had a copy of *The Economist*, which featured a provocative survey. It posed the question, "What's the probability of a third world war starting in the next 10 years?" At that time, people thought Slovakia was the most likely flashpoint, but Russia and America came in at 55 percent each. That scared me.

As a result, I met with John Mroz and Don Kendall, who used to run PepsiCo and was then chairman of EWI's board. John said, "If governments can't solve this problem between Russia and America, then let's bring in the private sector; let's start a private-sector Marshall Plan." We all agreed that this was an interesting line of thought. About a month later, I was in London in a cab with John and we both came to the conclusion that it

169

wasn't really a Marshall Plan, because the countries in Western Europe that received aid from the United States had already had experience with capitalism. They just needed seed money to get things started again after the war. However, Russia did not have that experience. Stalin and Molotov had rejected the Marshall Plan in 1947, and that was one of the opening salvos of the Cold War. Thus, we named our initiative the Kendall Russell Centre for Corporate Competitiveness and ran it out of EWI's Moscow office, which was relatively new at the time.

The EastWest Institute does a lot of very important things. One glance at their website (www.ewi.info) will give you an idea of its scope. The tabs on the left read: Worldwide Security, Preventive Diplomacy, Countering Violent Extremism, Weapons of Mass Destruction, Sustainable Human Security. At EastWest Institute, *mission critical* is more than a buzzword; it is literally true. Critical missions are what they work on every day. And that's why I believe John Mroz deserves the Nobel Peace Prize. I've been nominating him every year since January 2004. I understand he's been in the top 25, which isn't bad, considering he receives virtually no publicity. But I won't be satisfied until he wins.

The National Bureau of Asian Research

The National Bureau of Asian Research (NBR) came out of the late Senator Henry M. Jackson's work in international relations. "Scoop" was a great senator, perhaps the most distinguished and effective person who ever represented our state of Washington in Congress. As NBR co-founder Rich Ellings will tell you, Senator Jackson "believed that an urgent need existed for an institution that could tap the nation's best expertise to study Asia and Russia with U.S. national interests in mind. NBR was established in 1989 with two major grants from the Henry M. Jackson Foundation and the Boeing Company; both continue to provide critical core support for the organization to this day."

I've chaired NBR since 1993, and it's a great organization. They are different from EWI: Whereas EWI implements on the ground,

NBR is more focused on research—as the name suggests. Despite having a small staff, NBR carries great influence in key sectors of the academic community. NBR also has a network of influential people within the federal government; more than 30 senators and approximately 50 members of the House serve on the advisory board. They are regularly involved in advising on many different projects.

The main purpose of NBR is to write policy studies on major issues in Asia; we distribute these to leaders in our government to help them make policy decisions. For example, if the topic is the Taiwan Straits or North Korea, we'll bring in two or three top-level academics who are respected authorities on the subject and ask them to draft a position paper that can be used as a guide.

When General John Shalikashvili retired as chairman of the Joint Chiefs of Staff in 1997, he settled in Steilacoom, which is just south of Tacoma. Our local Congressman Norm Dicks alerted us about his proximity and we were lucky to secure the participation of General Shalikashvili on the boards of both Frank Russell Trust Company and NBR.

I first met Condoleeza Rice when she was teaching at Stanford. Prior to becoming Secretary of State, she served as National Security Advisor during President Bush's first term. It was during that time period when the General and I made an appointment to speak with her. We offered to put NBR's resources to work creating a full report on the security issues in Asia with executive summaries in each area that could be updated annually. Secretary Rice thought that would be a terrific idea. The NBR report measured almost two inches thick. But to me, the summaries were the key. I've always told associates, "Don't make the summary more than one page." That way, people reading it can quickly understand what the issues are. And it's easier to update and keep current.

The Pacific Health Summit

The idea for The Pacific Health Summit was sparked by a conversation with Lee Hartwell, the Nobel-Prize-winning director of the Fred Hutchinson Cancer Research Center in Seattle. Lee observed that, in spite of all the high-tech equipment we have today, 95 percent of medical attention is focused on existing problems—and then it's too late.

That was exactly what Jane experienced when she fell ill. No one had any idea she had cancer until the doctors observed a swelling in her neck. They checked it and confirmed it was cancer. She died 13 months later. I thought, using the latest technology, what if they had discovered that she did have some cancer five years before that? The odds of saving her life would have been so much better.

It seemed to me that one of the chief obstacles was the lack of communication between the many researchers working independently. I felt instinctively that it was a bit like the lack of coordination between the CIA and the FBI before September 11. In the medical arena, researchers compete for grants, funding, awards, and so forth. As a business innovator, of course I could understand the fear of sharing their proprietary results. But I also felt a burning personal need to tell this community that *life*—early detection and therefore the saving of life—is by far the most important outcome.

Our general idea was that we should bring together the head medical people throughout the Asia-Pacific region to talk about early detection. I mentioned this to the board at NBR, and we agreed that since none of us really knew anything about health care, we needed to work with the very best in the field. The obvious choice was Bill Gates, Sr.

I met with Bill and he liked the idea. He called me the next day and he suggested we co-chair The Pacific Health Summit together. Our chief role was raising funds to get the initiative going. Today, NBR sponsors and organizes the Summit, in conjunction with the Bill and Melinda Gates Foundation, Wellcome Trust, and the Fred Hutchinson Cancer Research Center. The list of supporters begins with the U.S. National Cancer Institute, and also includes corporate sponsors: GE Healthcare, Microsoft, Intel, Coca-Cola, GSK, Merck, Pfizer, Fujitsu, Sanofi Pasteur, PepsiCo, Swedish Medical Center, HP, Abbott Nutrition, Zimmer Gunsul Frasca, Miraca Holdings, and Duke Medicine.

The Summit takes place in Seattle each June. The first Summit in 2005 addressed the issues of disease prevention and early detection and treatment. In subsequent years, the Summit topics focused on early health, pandemic preparedness and prevention, global nutrition, and most recently, the problem of multi-drug-resistant tuberculosis. While the Summit originally focused on the Asia-Pacific region, it has since dispensed with any geographic limitations. For the 2009 Summit, invitations have gone out to delegates in 22 different countries.

The Business Humanitarian Forum

The Business Humanitarian Forum (BHF) is another entity that had its inception in the network of people that NBR brings together. In this case, the spark was a working lunch we had with William Cohen, who was then Secretary of Defense. This was in 1998. I invited the CEOs of 14 major corporations and we had a fascinating discussion about Asia and its economic and political problems. At one point, our focus turned to Indonesia, whose economy then was in dire straits after the currency crisis. In spite of all the intelligence and experience sitting around the table, nobody could suggest anything the U.S. government could do to help Indonesia. Finally, I piped up and said, "Well, if the governments can't solve it, get the private sector in." (I am always promoting the private sector because, when you think about it, private economic enterprise is what creates GDP, not the government.) It was gratifying when the CEO of UNOCAL responded, on the spot, with a major commitment to fund schools in Indonesia.

This brings us to Ambassador John Maresca, who had joined NBR's board in 1997 while he was working as senior vice president at UNOCAL. During his prior diplomatic career, John served as the U.S. representative to the Organization for Security and Cooperation in Europe (OSCE). He negotiated the two documents that formally ended the Cold War and was later sent as Special Envoy to open U.S. relations with the newly independent states from the former Soviet Union. He has also served as an Assistant Secretary of Defense. I met him in Geneva, as part of the follow-up to UNOCAL's grant for schools in Indonesia. We called a meeting that I co-chaired with John Whitehead, a former director of Goldman Sachs and the Deputy Secretary of State under George Schultz. The guest speaker was Robert Zoellick, who is currently president of the World Bank. (Bob and I served together on the board of NBR for nearly a decade.) It was this constellation of people—Maresca, Zoellick, Whitehead, and Russell—that led to the formation of The Business Humanitarian Forum.

Ambassador Maresca is the driving force. He is a Central Asia expert, and his vision is to "encourage private sector support and public-private sector cooperation for economic and human development in post-conflict areas and poor countries where investment is needed."

What he is doing is fantastic. For example, in Afghanistan, they didn't have any factories that make aspirin, or any other kind of medications for that matter. To remedy that, The Business Humanitarian Forum built the first generic-medicine manufacturing facility in Afghanistan, completed in 2005. The project brought together local ownership with funding, resources, and management skills provided by BHF and its partners.

The project might sound simple, but in fact was extremely difficult to execute. The European Generic Medicines Association donated the equipment, but then how do you get it to Afghanistan, let alone Kabul? Ambassador Maresca arranged a grant from the Deutsche Investitions und Entwicklungsgesellschaft, which is the government development bank, and they paid to ship it via DHL! But then you have the nightmare of how to get it to Kabul safely over rough roads that have potentially hostile people with guns waiting in ambush along the route. It took Jack at least six months, working through detail after detail after detail. But he succeeded. The project was rightly recognized by the Overseas Private Investment Corporation as its most innovative development project of the year. More importantly, the Afghan people had improved access to medicine, *and* they gained valuable experience in how to develop infrastructure. Unfortunately, the manufacturing facility had to suspend operations recently due to heightened security risks.

One Nation Brings Together Americans of Different Faiths

One Nation grew out of a thought I had in 2005. I noticed a survey that showed—even four years after 9/11—that 50 percent of Americans mistrusted Muslims. That worried me. If that perception were to continue, I was concerned that the world would probably end up having a 100-year war, Islam against Christianity. To help avoid that, we set up One Nation with a board of Muslims, Christians, and Jews. The mission is to try to educate Americans on Islam. The focus is squarely on America with the goal of correcting misperceptions that could lead to armed conflict.

That was my thought process. To build the organization I turned to Henry Izumizaki, who was already at The Russell Family Foundation. Henry had prior experience building a non-profit, as founding president of T.E.A.M.S. (Transformation through Education and Mutual Support), a California nonprofit organization dedicated to training grassroots leaders.

Henry recruited a first-class board of experienced and talented people. Over time, we learned that promoting effective person-to-person relationships coupled with community building is the best way to help accelerate changes in public misperceptions. The core of this strategy involves the engagement of individual Americans, philanthropic institutions and local and national organizations that promote broad-based civic engagement and public service among American Muslims, their neighbors and American society at-large.

One Nation is developing two different civic engagement models to help cultivate strong personal relationships among people from diverse communities across the country. We are doing this to help build more vibrant and inclusive communities that together will help build a more inclusive and pluralistic America.

The first model is called the Midsize City Franchise Model, which will bring together individuals and communities in medium-size cities across the U.S. The pilot project is in Tacoma, Washington, where One Nation has partnered with Habitat for Humanity to develop and help finance 12 new homes, built by volunteers from multi-faith communities representing several groups of Christians, Muslims, Jews, Buddhists, and Native Americans.

The other model is the Large City Franchise Model, which will bring together individuals, communities, institutions and organizations in America's largest cities. The initial project is in Chicago, Illinois, where more than 400,000 American Muslims live in the metropolitan area. One Nation has designed a multi-tiered approach that includes an online film competition, a series of community dialogues, and community investment funding.

And that's just the beginning. Both of these models are being developed to be replicable, scalable and locally fundable so that they can be easily implemented in cities across the U.S.

A Child's Right

My most recent project is supporting an initiative called "A Child's Right." It is a small organization with a focused mission of bringing clean drinking water to children. Economists estimate that there are 1.1 billion people worldwide who do not have access to clean water, and the brunt of the impact falls on children. As A Child's Right founder Eric Stowe explains, "Of the three million people who die every year due to waterborne diseases caused by unclean water, 90 percent are children under the age of five. These diseases are the single biggest threat to children the world over."

Eric's solution is as local as you can get. He identifies specific communities that need clean water and puts together a crew to install water-purification systems that include filtration units and storage containers. He also provides extensive hygiene education, targeting orphanages, street shelters, schools, and children's hospitals.

He's gone out to a wide variety of places in the world— Cambodia, Sri Lanka, Nepal, Vietnam. Recently he's done installations throughout western China and now he's working in the most densely populated part of eastern China. Besides being a great, honest person, Eric Stowe is making a big, direct impact on human lives. I'm proud to be associated with his efforts.

■ ■ ■

As you can see, I'm having fun. When I look at my life today, I estimate I spend 40 percent of my time on business, 40 percent on travel, and then 20 percent on free time. As far as I'm concerned, no matter how old I get, I'll always devote almost half of my time to business efforts. There's no word like *retirement* in my vocabulary. There's no need for it. That's because I enjoy what I do.

That's my final bit of advice for you: Whatever you do, have fun. There's no time in life for negative thoughts; always look to the positive side of things. Go through life with a smile. Of course everyone encounters personal tragedies and losses. But life goes on. So make the most of every opportunity that comes your way.

Note

1. Robert H. Bates, *The Love of Mountains Is Best: Climbs and Travels from K2 to Kathmandu* (Portsmouth: Peter E. Randall, 1994).

Key Points from Chapter 10

1. Have fun as much as possible, both in and outside of work.
2. Occasional breaks, like the Russell sabbatical program afforded, are great investments; they enhance productivity and seed innovation.
3. Try to do work that you really enjoy. Stick with clients that you respect and respect you; otherwise, it's hard to go the extra mile and produce exceptional results.
4. Philanthropy is fun. Do as much of it as you can.
5. Stay positive: Things work out over time, so keep moving forward.

About the Authors

George F. Russell, Jr.

Internationally known as an advocate for narrowing the gap between the "haves" and the "have nots," George Russell focuses on a number of challenges: the promotion of globalization, the destruction of nuclear waste, strengthening U.S.-Russian relations, ground-level humanitarian projects, and bridging the current divide between Muslims and non-Muslims in America.

Starting in 1958, George built Frank Russell Company from a small, regional mutual fund company into one of the world's leading investment advisory firms. He served as chairman from 1958 until the firm was sold to Northwestern Mutual Life in 1999. Today, the company guides over 1,900 clients in 44 countries with assets exceeding more than $2.4 trillion, and manages $171 billion in funds. The company name is commonly recognized by the prominent stock market index, the Russell 2000, which is one of a large number of Russell indexes around the world.

A native of Tacoma, Washington, George pioneered the business of pension fund consulting in the late 1960s. He is a well-known advocate of diversified global investing and, along with Warren Buffett, was named in 1993 by *Pensions & Investments* as one of the four most influential people in the world of institutional investing, in addition to numerous other awards including the Lillywhite Award from the Employee Benefits Research Council for outstanding lifetime contributions to enhancing Americans' economic security, the CFA Institute's Thomas L. Hansberger Leadership in Global Investing Award in October 2008, and the Woodrow Wilson Award for Public Service in June 2009.

Currently, George co-chairs the EastWest Institute (EWI); is chairman of One Nation, a project working to change the perceptions of Islam and Muslims in America; and chairman of The National Bureau of Asian Research, and under their name chairs The Pacific Health Summit. He is chairman of Nuclear Fuel Cycle Technologies, Inc., The Russell Family Foundation, and Threshold Group, a multi-client family office dedicated to private wealth management and comprehensive, fully integrated services. He is on the Leadership Council for the Initiative for Global Development and a member of the International Advisory Board for the University for Peace, which supports peace and security objectives of the United Nations. George is honorary co-chairman of the Business Humanitarian Forum and a board member of Woods Hole Oceanographic Institution.

Michael Sheldon

Michael Sheldon worked at Frank Russell Company from 1993 to 1999, writing marketing materials and helping George Russell draft articles and client communications. He co-founded XMedia Communications in 1999 to provide marketing copywriting, creative content, and strategy to a diverse clientele that ranges from startups to global corporations in a variety of industries. He is currently at work on a new book, entitled *Business Is Good: How BIG Writing Can Advance Your Career and Make Any Organization More Productive.*

Index

Key points:
  creativity, 75
  credit sharing, 107
  fun, 177
  hard work, 92
  hiring of smart people, 54
  integrity, 12
  luck, 125
  persistence, 29
  risks, 158
  transitions, 141
Kiriyenko, Sergei, 148, 149
Kirschman, Jeannette, 78

L
Layman, Ralph, 148–149, 150
Lend Lease, 151
Lert, Randy, 69, 74, 89, 134
Lichtenberg, Joan, 82
Lighthouse Christian School, 137
Ling, Jim, 18–19, 109, 110
Ling-Temco-Vought, 18–20
Lothrop, Dick, 16–17, 19, 57, 61, 68, 164
Lothrop, Shirley, 17
Love of Mountains Is Best, The (Bates), 161
Luck, recognizing of, 109–125
  decision-making and, 111–116
  key points, 125
  Russell Indexes and, 116–124
  skill and, 122–123
Lynch, Peter, 94

M
Manager research, hiring
  practices and, 36–40

Mann-Russell Electronics, 14–15
Maresca, John, 173–174
Markowitz, Harry, 32, 44
Martin, Jim, 68
Mbeki, Thabo, 148
McDonald, Jim, 89, 91
McLaughlin, Ish, 97
M-cubed process, 64–65
Melnikoff, Meyer, 58–59
Mistakes, 98–104
Modern Portfolio Theory, 32, 59, 60
Mohamad, Mahathir bin, 148–149
Money Flood, The (Clowes), 20
Money Market Directory, 20–21
Monsanto, 101
Montague, Charles, 93
Mountaineering, 3–5, 79–80, 160–161
Mroz, John, 145–146, 158, 168, 169–170
Multiperiod stochastic optimization, 152–154
Murray, Roger, 44
Mutual funds, early investing in, 16, 17–20

N
National Bureau of Asian Research, 170–171
NCREIF Property Index (NPI), 59–60
New York Stock Exchange seat, 28, 81, 144
Nielsen, Brandy, 68, 69–70